TOWN GOVERNMENT IN VERMONT

TOWN GOVERNMENT IN VERMONT

or

"Making Democracy 'Democ' "

James P. Taylor

ANDREW E. NUQUIST

McCullough Professor
of Political Science
University of Vermont

Government Research Center
University of Vermont, Burlington, Vt.
1964

TO EDITH

Contents

SECTION III
SPECIAL DISTRICTS 131

SECTION IV
THE SUFFRAGE AND REPRESENTATION 155

SECTION V
CONSERVATION PROBLEMS 171

SECTION VI
THE COUNTY AND ITS PROBLEMS 199

Preface

The material for this study has been collected over a period of almost a quarter of a century. During these years, hundreds of town officials and students have both contributed facts and have been subjected to interpretations growing out of the information supplied. It is impossible to recall and thank them all, and unfair to choose a few. Consequently, my obligations and thanks go to all of those persons without whose help this publication could not have appeared. Mr. Robert B. Mitchell, Editor of the Rutland Daily Herald, initiated the series of articles upon which the present revision is based, and in addition, made arrangements for others to write articles with a bearing on town government. A long series of state officials have given of their time and tempers, and contributed much printed material to help me pinpoint facts and interpretations. The University of Vermont has granted a sabbatical year which has meant the boon of enough time to write, the lack of which would have prevented the appearance of this volume. Thanks should be given to Mrs. Marie Schwenn for her translating and transcribing what passes for my handwriting. My wife, Edith W. Nuquist, has borne the brunt of typing and revising the final draft, in an effort to bring to fruition the years of study and the weeks of absences spent in town officers' schools. All husbands and wives in similar situations know what I mean and how much she has helped. My hope is that those who have so cheerfully aided me will not feel that I have distorted or twisted their ideas beyond recognition. In any case, they know that the fault was not theirs but mine in not being more observant and careful.

ANDREW E. NUQUIST

Burlington, Vermont
October 1963

Introduction

In the fall of 1946, Mr. Robert B. Mitchell, Editor of the Rutland Daily Herald in Rutland, Vermont, wrote to me asking if I would write a short weekly column concerning town government in Vermont. Neither he nor I envisaged the amount of material which would come out of this simple request. What had been intended, I am sure, was a series of ten or twelve columns at the most, but with a few interruptions, they ran until 1948, when with the seventy-sixth article the series came to an end. The subject matter having been expanded greatly and the discussion having been more comprehensive than was intended originally, the material engendered a considerable interest. In the years since the series appeared many requests have been received for the reprint of the series, or for their appearance in book form. Many promises have been made and the hope expressed that this would soon be a reality. At long last the book is written.

The background for *Town Government in Vermont* stems from my early days as an Instructor at the University of Vermont. During the first year of my residence in the state I made the acquaintance of the late James P. Taylor, who was and for many years had been the Executive Secretary of the Vermont State Chamber of Commerce. Mr. Taylor was a remarkable individual — a publicist of no mean ability and a person who loved the state of Vermont to a greater degree than most people realized. He had spent his active working life here, first as a teacher in Vermont Academy at Saxtons River where he originated several programs which are still practiced there, and some, such as Dartmouth's Winter Carnival, which have been copied in other states and other institutions. Among the projects that Jim Taylor fostered was the laying out and the building of the Long Trail in Vermont — the Long Trail later became a portion of the Appalachian Trail that extends from Georgia to Maine. Mr. Taylor was a fervent believer in concrete highways, and in an expanded highway program. He had a great deal to do with the perfecting of town reporting in this state and elsewhere, and he originated Town Report Contests, which have been copied widely, and are now found in one form or another in almost every section of the United States.

It was Jim Taylor who came to me one day and asked if I would be interested in doing some work on Town Reports; upon my affirmative answer there then began an active and burdensome relationship that ended only with Jim Taylor's death in 1950. The first result of my answer was that I was taken all over the state to meetings which had already been scheduled and which Jim thought I should attend — there were meetings for mayors, for town managers, for business leaders, for state officers, for political figures, or for all combined. The inevitable opening statement, until I had made the rounds and was known at least by sight to most of the men, and made in his own inimitable style which is not here reproduced was, "This young pup wants to learn something about local government and since you know all about it, it is time you start teaching him a part of what you know." Along with this introduction was the well-known aside of his, "Now just among us girls," and comments about academic long-hairs leaving the ivory towers to mingle "with us common folks." In spite of these minor embarrassments, this academican valued the opportunity to become acquainted with those who move in and control state affairs, and to get the inside story of how government is run. The men were interesting, the contacts pleasant, and the friendships lasting.

Payment for this instructive and enjoyable travel about Vermont was exacted in long evenings of work in Jim's dusty, cluttered, and ill-lighted office. There at various times I worked with and under the supervision of Warren R. (Dick) Dodge, Jim Taylor, members of the State Chamber of Commerce, and occasionally an out-of-state visitor, as we read and commented on Town Reports and evaluated them for the annual Town Report contest. We would also discuss Jim's latest "idea" and review the comments and letters this idea had engendered from Governors and public officials from many states.

Within a year I began attending the Town Officers' Schools — a series of meetings for town officials which were held each fall throughout Vermont. I learned the importance of getting these schools organized so that they would not interfere with corn-cutting and yet be held before the fall rains began. Mostly I was driven to them by the late Raymond L. Soule, then assessor of Burlington. At every crossroad I heard the story of its history, when passing country homes the background of the farm, and when crossing abandoned railroad lines I heard tales of Mr. Soule's experience as a salesman when he had had to hire liveries to get out to the country stores. This would lead to stories of the University of Vermont and the eccentrics who made the school a locus for the best sort of learning, and to reminiscences of its graduates. The homes of graduates and classmates were pointed out and now and then we stopped to pass the time of day. Coming home from a meeting we would often take back roads, which to a prairie-reared newcomer appeared impassable or downright dangerous, in order to see some scenic or historic site. We always returned safely, and the next trip was more meaningful because of the side trips — Mr. Soule's continuing stories now had background.

Once in a while, after the hearty noon meals served for the large sum of fifty cents by the ladies of some church or organization, the leaders of the school would pile into one or two cars and drive out along some rural road for a few minutes away from the crowds. Then amidst much chaffing and stories of the Tunbridge Fair, a pint of "medicine" would circulate the group and a wee nip would be taken to nerve the participants for the afternoon sessions. The town officials would oftentimes go to their cars for a bit of communion with the cup that cheers, but very rarely and to the acute embarrassment of fellow townsmen, was it taken too liberally.

At times the distance, the weather, or a combination of the two necessitated an overnight stop at one of the small village inns — in the days before the current tourist boom this could be a memorable experience. After a communal meal with the participants of the town officers' school who had stayed over, what evenings those were! They were enlightening, light-hearted, and full of reminiscences. Dick Dodge, Jim Taylor, Benjamin Gates of the always busy artistic hands, Judge Erwin M. Harvey of the walrus moustache, Raymond Soule, George Amidon, David Anderson, Clyde Coffrin, — all were raconteurs of no mean ability and each strove to outdo the others. One memorable story concerned the two best authorities on municipal law in the state, Judge Harvey and Theodore Hopkins, then Burlington City Attorney. Late one evening a mutual friend had gone to Hopkin's office in the City Hall looking for the two men. Both were on their hands and knees arguing over an open law book on the floor before them. Every table, chair, desk, and most of the floor was covered with opened statutes and court reports. The two old cronies had been arguing a nice point of municipal law since early afternoon and had not noted the passage of time. This story carried a real connotation to those who knew the portly judge and the courtly, Vandyked Hopkins.

In September 1941, the town officers' schools were not the same. Dick Dodge had been called into active duty and someone had to read his previously prepared speech, but somehow it lacked the fire and authority of Dick's presentation. The town officers were worried as the war clouds darkened and their sons left home for training in Louisiana, and elsewhere. Gasoline rationing prevented travel; the town officers' schools had to be suspended for the duration. During the War years Jim Taylor's office functioned by mail and as an information and collection center. At any hour of the day or evening my phone would ring and Jim would appear to talk about some new gadget or idea to help improve town government. The first post-war town officers' school was held in 1946. Some of the older men had passed on, and even Jim Taylor was no longer the dynamo he had been. In the last year or two of his life increasing demands upon my time led to a partial shifting of Jim's "pressure" to my then new colleague, Professor Rolf N.B. Haugen. The division of work made life less strenuous than if either of us had had to bear the brunt of proposals from Jim Taylor's fertile mind.

The articles for the Rutland Herald were written under these post-war circumstances. In their revised form, as now presented in *Town Government in Vermont,* the most remarkable fact is the number of reforms, changes, and improvements that are seen to have taken place since the first writing in 1946-48. Quietly, each year, the state is catching up to the proposals made so long ago by the men listed above. In many ways this present study is a report on dying or departed practices, and may well be a swan song for the type of government it describes. Time *does* bring changes, and the observer can only hope that the emerging form of local government can inspire the best efforts of its practitioners in the way the old Town Meeting did for its leading lights.

SECTION I

Town Government In General

CHAPTER 1

Origins and Problems of Town Government

It is the purpose of this publication, which is a revision of a series of articles, to discuss some of the problems of Vermont towns. The writer firmly believes that when people know the facts and their consequences there is little doubt that these persons will act wisely and well. This country developed and became a great nation on the common sense of the individual citizen. Those who question the ability of the people to handle their own affairs are betrayers of the principles for which our young men and women died during two world wars. The burden of proof lies with the detractors of democratic government.

A little over two hundred years ago adventurous men from other parts of the British colonies began to push into the territory that is now Vermont for the purpose of settling and making homes for their families. Coming mainly from the rest of the area now known as New England, they brought with them the form of government to which they were accustomed. Because of frontier conditions and the desire to cast off the old restraints from which they had fled, the Vermont pioneers maintained a distinction between church and state. This had not been the case in Massachusetts. Thus it was that there was more truly a democracy in Vermont than in most of the other colonies.

New England town government began within a few years of the founding of the settlements around Boston.[1] The General Court had been faced with the problem of controlling the expanding population of that growing colony, and the offshoots of the parental settlements on the Charles were becoming numerous and self-sufficient.

---

1 See Sly, John F., *Town Government in Massachusetts*, 1620-1930, Cambridge, 1930.

The question of what to do with these people was solved by giving each settlement the right to organize and govern its own community as a town, using the forms prevalent in the older areas, which in turn had come over from the English parish.

Every week, or month, all the freemen of the town were supposed to assemble in the Meeting House to transact such business as was meet and proper. Even at that time there was considerable absenteeism, and the descendents of those freemen have been following the precedent thus set ever since. As the activities of the town increased people no longer wished to do all the work themselves. This resulted in the appointment and then the election of a committee of "select men" to act between meetings. Consequently, these town meetings were held at longer and longer intervals, until today the Town Meeting is held once a year. Only rarely does it assemble in special session.

When the informal beginning had been legalized, the Town Meeting became the formal legislative body for the community. All powers of control were lodged in the Meeting, and it was empowered to choose such officers as the needs of the times demanded. Here in Vermont, the inhabitants early decided that all adult males were to be free and privileged to attend and to vote at the Town Meetings.[2] This state was thus the first to grant full suffrage without property and religious requirements.

---

2 The first constitution of Vermont stated: — That all men are born equally free and independent, and have certain natural, inherent and inalienable rights, amongst which are the enjoying and defending life and liberty; acquiring, possessing and protecting property, and pursuing and obtaining happiness and safety. Therefore, no male person, born in this country, or brought from over sea, ought to be holden by law, to serve any person, as a servant, slave or apprentice, after he arrives to the age of eighteen years, unless they are bound by their own consent, after they arrive to such age, or bound by law, for the payment of debts, damages, fines, costs, or the like. (Chapter I, Section I of the Vermont *Constitution of 1777*.)

To complete this granting of rights the document also went on to say: — Every man of the full age of twenty-one years, having resided in this State for the space of one whole year, next before the election of representatives, and who is of a quiet and peaceable behaviour, and will take the following oath (or affirmation) shall be entitled to all the privileges of a freeman of this State. (Chapter II, Section VI of the Vermont *Constitution of 1777*.)

For more than two hundred years the citizens of Vermont have met to discuss their local problems. Every first Tuesday in March the annual Town Meeting now formulates the policies of the town for the next year, and instructs the officers whom the meeting has chosen how far they can go in the expenditure of money and in the conduct of the town's business. In recent years there has been a steady decline in participation until in some towns there are scarcely more persons present than the officers who are required to be there. Since self-government can continue only when citizens participate, the future of town government in Vermont has been questioned by many. Suggestions for compulsory attendance have been proposed, but this could have no permanent or useful results.

Regardless of the relatively small attendance at Town Meeting the caliber of town government is usually reasonably effective. It is probably due to the unstinting efforts of those who serve as officers that this is true, and not to the rank and file of the citizenry. Thus, the Town Meeting remains the one place in the United States where the individual can participate directly in the formation of public policy through legislative action. The question today is whether this form of pure democracy meets the needs of modern living.

The basic unit of local government in the United States is either the town or the county. Other than in New England, sixteen states make use of town government or its weaker sister — the township. Except for the state of Washington, these other states are in the northeast and they were settled early by persons originally stemming from New England. In none of these sixteen states is the town, or township, as the case may be, very active or important. The areas go through the motions of self-government, but in all but a few places it is merely a nodding acquaintance with the real thing.[3] Thus it is that the town form of government retains real significance in New England alone.

Most of the other 28 states of the Union, following the form which originated in the old plantation south, make the county the

---

3 In Minnesota, for example, town governments have steadily lost powers and even a separate existence since the Depression, while in Iowa, township governments have been abolished and their governmental functions transferred to the county.

basic unit of their local government. The 3043 counties in the 50 states average about 960 square miles in area, as compared with an average of 36 to 40 square miles for the town or township. The average county population in the United States is about 61,000, while towns in Vermont vary from 38 to 13,002 in population. There is no real legislative branch in the county; hence few, if any, local laws. There is no real executive branch; elected county officers administer state laws. The judicial branch in the county consists of judges who administer state laws. The county then tends to be merely a unit for administering state laws. Although there are counties in Vermont they should not be confused with those of most other states; the 14 counties in this state have no real functions to perform except to act as judicial and election districts.

The county as a form of government, as found in the United States, should not be considered as the solution for the inadequacies of present local government, or as a replacement for the town. Students and observers of the county say that the counties are frequently too small in wealth and area for an economic and efficient administration of local services to their citizens. Since the same human needs are present everywhere, the critics immediately jump to the conclusion that because the town is even smaller in area it ought to be liquidated at once. These critics suggest no government form to replace the town.

A town in New England, in contrast to the above mentioned counties, does have the privilege of enacting legislation.[4] Through its Town Meeting it formulates and executes its own policies, within the limits prescribed by the state legislature — a body not unresponsive to the wishes of the towns of Vermont. An observer of local

---

4 On the municipal level the town meeting performs the legislative function. It is the legislative body. Its duty is to enact such laws as towns are permitted to adopt for their regulation and for the public welfare of the inhabitants. Its votes in municipal government correspond to those of the General Court in the state government and of the Congress in the national government. Once the town meeting has adjourned, the administration and enforcement of its laws lie in the hands of the various administrative officers, of which most towns have a large number. Tilden, Robert J.; *How Town Meeting Functions*, p 1, an article appearing first in the *Falmouth Enterprise* (Massachusetts) April 12, 1957.

government in Vermont has said that there is "an awful lot of local government carried on at the local level."[5]   In the other 16 states which have town government the tendency is for the town to mirror the ineffectiveness of the county.

After two centuries of local government the ordinary town in Vermont remains small. The ten smallest towns in the state had fewer than 100 inhabitans each in 1960, their combined population being 661 persons. Stratton with 38 persons is the smallest town in the state, and Bennington town with 13,002 persons is the largest. The latter figure is 342 times larger than the former. In spite of this discrepancy in numbers each town has one representative in the lower House in Montpelier, and each is required by law to have the same officials and the same form of government, unless they choose to adopt the Town Manager system.

There are today 238 towns in Vermont (two less than in 1937, when the General Assembly "deorganized" the towns of Glastonbury and Somerset), and 8 cities. The predominately rural character of the town is one explanation for the continued existence of so many small divisions of Vermont local government — divisions which reflect the state's population pattern of 150 years ago. Another explanation is that no small town has ever willingly surrendered its existence or its "right" to representation in the state legislature equal to that enjoyed by the larger towns.

Town government is thus a major part of the very fabric of Vermont state government and assumes an importance that cannot be ignored. If the town is unable to satisfy its citizens in giving services the mere fact that is exists is of little more than historical importance. A growing recognition of the problems facing the towns in Vermont is bringing forth efforts to ease their burdens. Under the laws of Vermont several towns may combine to hire a joint town manager[6] " . . . who shall have general supervision of the affairs of the town, be the administrative head of all departments of

---

5 *Rutland Daily Herald,* 1954. An editorial citing and commending the series of articles on town officers by Miss Betty McWhorter.

6   24 VSA §   1232

This means Title twenty-four, Section 1232, of the *Vermont Statutes Annotated,* which is published in nine volumes. This citation happens to be in volume seven. All future citations of this publication will follow this form.

the town government and shall be responsible for the efficient administration thereof."[7] Although this provision has been on the statute books since 1917, it was not until the spring of 1963, that the towns of Bethel and Randolph agreed to hire the same manager. There is no loss of town identity and each town can still make its own decisions as to what it wants to do.

Over the years there have been those who would go further than voluntary cooperation and who advocated combining the small towns, or incorporating them into larger towns, in order to create larger and more efficient units of government. Beyond some very tentative suggestions no concrete proposals were forthcoming. However, in 1963, the General Assembly of Vermont took an unanticipated step in this direction. It passed legislation which permits towns to combine. The action is to be wholly voluntary, even though there had been a gesture toward making it mandatory.[8]

Mere combination into larger units of administrative areas would not guarantee citizen interest in local government. Without this interest there could be no lasting improvement. Self-government is just that, and can be nothing else. The proper practices and right answers for Vermont are found in no school or book, although hints may be found or suggestions sought elsewhere. And so every plan or proposal for improvement or reform in local practices in Vermont runs into the wall of hard fact that the final answer in these matters must be found at home, following careful discussion and the experiences of trial and error.

Concomitant with the necessity for citizen interest and participation is the recognition of, and use of, the special training and abilities of those resident in the community. Those who have some particular bent of interest or training should follow their specialties. The traditional attitude of the jack-of-all-trades frame of mind says that anyone is capable of filling any office and peforming any task well. The pressing activities of modern life have proved this to be a fallacious concept. No one person in a town can know all the

7   24 VSA § 1235.

8   No. 146 of the *Acts of 1963*. This citation is a short form and will be used hereafter in this Book. It stands for *Acts and Resolves Passed by the General Assembly of the State of Vermont at the Forty-seventh Biennial Session, 1963.* For the earliest publications of the State the citation will substitute the word *Laws* for *Acts*.

answers, but many a citizen can know some one phase thoroughly and be aware of the existence of several others. A few fortunate persons may even know several phases well, but ordinarily, specialization is accepted as a part of modern life. The mutual sharing of specialties at the Town Meeting will make for greater success in local activities.

Rather than abjectly surrendering to despair, the townspeople need to foster the idea that each citizen is responsible for some one phase of government and should cooperate with others who have similar interests in the study of these problems. For example, in past years there has been a continuous series of hearings and meetings on flood control, milk control, stream pollution, and many other items. The individual citizen could not possibly have attended them all. But many people did go to at least one hearing and learned much. These interested and informed persons should be the center of activity in their given fields in their towns. The mutual sharing of information, a sharing which inevitably must change some fixed patterns, is the basis of better local government.

Town officers who have the support of alert constituents do better work than those who have no help. Interested citizens and officials are the best source of material for higher posts in state government; those who have been trained in local and state affairs are better equipped to fill national posts. This training, supported by informed citizens, will tend to prevent the "little accidents" in politics which are so costly when unworthy persons reach high office. Full, alert, and informed interest at the town level and in Town Meeting are of far more import than the geographical dimensions of local governmental areas, but they are not mutually exclusive.

CHAPTER 2

The Town Meeting and The Warning

There was once a time when governmental activities in a Vermont town consisted of little more than an attempt to raise the money to construct trails through the forest, and to maintain a school. Today it takes pages and pages, and many chapters of the VERMONT STATUTES ANNOTATED to state the rights, duties, and privileges of the towns and town officers. The laws tell what matters may be handled by the Town Meeting, the number of officials to be elected and/or appointed, and regulate the minutiae of public government.[1] These laws provide for two major categories of town activities — policy decisions and the administrative and housekeeping duties. Decisions in both categories must be made by the Town Meeting, which means that any decision is likely to reflect a confusion arising from an inability to distinguish between what is town business and what is the business of specific officials.

The State *Constitution* provides that the General Assembly shall enact legislation and gives it the right "to constitute towns . . ."[2] Under this authority the laws which authorize the town to act really become mandates from the state which must be observed. It is at the Town Meeting that the townsman carries out his duties and privileges, as authorized by the legislature, and enacts such laws as he is permitted to adopt for the regulation of town business and for the public welfare of the town's inhabitants.

The annual Town Meeting of Vermont towns is held on the first Tuesday in March, pursuant to the laws of the state,[3] but as many other special meetings as may be necessary may be called by

---

1 In this connection see specifically Title 24 VSA, Vol. 7, pp 329-589.
2 Section 6, of Chapter II.
3 24 VSA § 702.

the selectmen, or must be called when five per cent of the voters of the town so request by petition.[4]

Every Town Meeting must be warned, that is, a notice of the date and time of the meeting and a statement of all matters upon which a vote is to be taken, must be placed in at least three places in the town where people congregate or would normally pass by, and/or be published in a newspaper of general circulation in the town.[5] The law requires the posting or publication to be not less than twelve days nor more than twenty days before the meeting, and that it shall be done by the selectmen, or any of them, or in their absence, by the town clerk. Those towns that have adopted the Australian ballot follow different rules, since the requirement here is that the posting shall be done not less than twenty-one nor more than twenty-eight days before the meeting.[6]

The selectmen, or any one or more of them still in office, are responsible for seeing that the original copy of the warning is filed with the town clerk and the document recorded before it is posted.[7] The selectmen may put anything in the warning they desire, as long as it is legally possible to vote on the matter. They may put such additional articles in the warning as the citizens may request and they are willing to add, and they must put in those articles that are requested by petition of the required five per cent of the voters.[8]

Every item that is to be voted on must be specifically stated in the warning in such a way that there is no doubt as to its meaning. Long ago the Supreme Court of Vermont said, "The warning should indicate the subject for consideration with reasonable certainty, and in such a manner that no person interested could be misled in respect to the proposition to be submitted for the consideration and action of the town. . . ."[9]

Many people become impatient at the requirements for detailed listing of all actions taken, but it is a wise precaution. It represents the tried and true belief that no one can act wisely or well

4   24   VSA   §   705.
5   24   VSA   §   705.
6   17   VSA   §   577, *Op. Attorney General*, No. 256, Jan. 30, 1958, and No. 154 of the *Acts of 1959*.
7   24   VSA   §   706.
8   24   VSA   §   705.
9   35   *Vermont Reports* 219, at p. 222. (1860).

without the facts. If an issue could be brought up without prior
notice, it might be passed on the basis of incomplete information
and to the grave detriment of the town. If, on the other hand, notice
is given ahead of time no one can say that he did not know what
was coming up, and no one has the excuse of not having had a
chance to know or to look up the facts. In this way the whole community is protected.

However, a condensed or short form of warning, which is
probably legal, has sometimes been used by some towns, but its
use is not wise for it presumes that everyone is thoroughly aware
of the matters to be discussed, and that is an assumption that is
easily rebutted. For their own protection the selectmen should be
careful to state every article fully and clearly, so that the citizens
have a "reasonable certainty" that they know what business is to
be transacted. In this connection it is important that the town is
not misled by the old catch-all phrase, "and to transact such other
business as may legally come before the town," which is usually
placed as the last article at the end of the warning. This phrase
is not sufficient to permit a vote which will bind the town. The
phrase does permit full and free discussion on any matter which
anyone wishes to present, but votes taken thereunder are not upon
issues which were "indicated . . . . with reasonable certainty," and
as such are not binding. Judge Ervin M. Harvey, former State
Commissioner of Taxes, used to say that the only votes upon this
article that were valid were a rising vote of thanks to the ladies who
had prepared the noon meal, or for thanking the moderator for
having done a fine job.

The list of valid articles in the warning is a long one. In addition to those desired by the selectmen or the townspeople, there
are many that must be voted on at stated intervals by statutory requirement, and others that may be, when requested. A series of
these taken from the VERMONT STATUTES ANNOTATED will
illustrate the complexity of local activities.

First, there must be an article calling for the election of town
officers.[10]   This should be a complete listing rather than merely
calling for the vote "on the usual officers." In every case where
there is an elected board of officers the term of each officer is three

---

10   24   VSA   §   711.

years, with one only being elected annually, except in cases of death or resignation, when more may be chosen. In addition to the selectman and the lister whose terms have expired, one or more extra selectmen and one or more extra listers may be voted into office, if there is an article to that effect in the warning.[11] The town has to vote on whether the selectmen are to appoint one or more road commissioners, or are to be responsible for the roads themselves.[12]

All money for town expenses must be voted specifically, an action which requires an adequate article in the warning; and the vote is to be on a "specific sum or rate per cent on a dollar of the grand list."[13] The proposed tax rate must be accepted, changed, or rejected by the citizens in Town Meeting. Furthermore, they must decide whether or not they will undertake projects that will cause the town to go into debt. If they so decide, they must fix the amount, the term, and the method of repayment. The town officers are required to keep the total indebtedness of the town within the legal limit of ten times the grand list.

The three town auditors are supposed to have taken the entire town program into account when they make their annual report on the legality of the town expenditures. Their Town Report, published and in the hands of the citizens in time for Town Meeting, is expected to contain the facts the citizens need to make informed decisions. Sometimes there are unplanned delays, or the Report is so disorganized that it is of little value, and hence policy decisions are made with inadequate information.

Every even year, 1962, for example, the selectmen must insert an item in the warning calling for a vote on the question of whether or not the town will authorize the auditors to call on the state auditor to send someone to audit the own's books. If the town votes yes, the auditors must call on the state auditor for such help.[14] In any year the selectmen may, and if 4 per cent of the voters for governor in the last election so petition, must, insert in the warning for a regular or special meeting an article calling for the employ-

---

11   24   VSA   §   714.

12   24   VSA   §   715, 716.

13   24   VSA   §   717.

14   24   VSA   §   1692.

ment of a public accountant or auditor to audit the town books.[15]
This vote does not relieve the town of the duty to elect the town
auditors called for by law.[16]

The town must vote on the method of poll tax collection, with
the item clearly warned.[17] The same kind of article must be given
for a vote on whether or not there is to be a discount allowed on
taxes paid on time,[18] and whether there shall be payment of taxes
by installments.[19] The statutes give the form for this in the warning,
and also provide for the voting of discounts on the installments.[20]

It there is an item in the warning to that effect, the town can
vote salaries to its officers, or leave the exact amounts up to the
selectmen to determine, if the meeting does not care to set the
figures itself.[21] The fiscal year may be set to close at any date between the 31st of December, and the 31st of January, and the
date so fixed is to stand until it is rescinded by a vote of the town in
a meeting duly warned.[22]

In functioning as a governmental unit the town has to decide
when and where to lay out, build, and maintain highways and roads,
and at the same time cooperate with the state in its effort to improve the network of state highways. Administratively, the selectmen and one or more highway commissioners are required to perform these tasks. The town may vote to make the overseer of the
poor an independent officer subject to the supervision of the selectmen,[23] or may vote to permit the selectmen to serve in that capacity
themselves. The town determines the broad policies for the care
and keeping of its poor and unfortunate. The statutes provide that
a first and perhaps a second constable must be chosen[24] to help
prevent breaches of the peace in the town and to bring in the lawbreakers. It is also the task of the constable to carry legal instru-

---

15 24 VSA § 1691.
16 *Ibid.*
17 32 VSA § 5017, of §§ 5013 - 5023.
18 32 VSA § 4773.
19 32 VSA § 4871.
20 32 VSA § 4876.
21 24 VSA §§ 932, 933.
22 24 VSA § 1683.
23 24 VSA § 873.
24 24 VSA § 711 (9).

ments which have been issued, and to make proper returns as to their disposition. He also presides at the ballot box at elections.[25] A legal agent to hire counsel to handle the town's suits must be chosen. The decisions concerning these officers can often determine the trend of the town's reputation.

Before the close of the town meeting additional officers must be appointed by the selectmen — three fence viewers to help the townspeople maintain neighborly relations by keeping their fence lines in order and in the proper location, a tree warden to keep the public shade trees in proper condition for town beautification, and cemetery commissioners who are to maintain the cemeteries. The latter are legally to invest the funds left in trust for the upkeep of the graves and grounds, and to use the income for the purposes specified in the trusts.

The town is required to have a fireproof vault. If none is provided, there should be an article calling for a vote for the purchase or construction of such a vault or safe.[26] Frequently this item has been neglected until a fire has destroyed much or all of the town records, and then the vote is taken when it is too late.

A detailed portion of the statutes[27] requires that there be an item in the warning every year calling for a vote on the sale of spirituous liquors in the town, and on whether licenses for the sale of malt and vinous beverages shall be granted. This one item brings out more votes than any other article in the warning.

On the question of voting to permit Sunday amusements, the law clearly states that if the town has voted on an article in the warning to permit such amusements, this vote shall stand until there is a request by petition of five per cent of the voters for a new vote on the matter. The same is true of a negative vote, which stands until there is a petition for a new vote, and the required article has been placed in the warning.[28] Although permissible amusements have been expanded in recent years, this portion of the statutes is still considered of much importance by local townspeople. In 1963, the legislature refused to permit the towns to vote

---

25   17 VSA   §   1002.
26   24 VSA   §   1178.
27   7 VSA   §§   161 - 167.
28   13 VSA   §§   3301 - 3305.

on whether they would allow Sunday dancing, although the proposed law made it entirely voluntary with any town which wished to take action.

Finally, in addition to all this, the town must build, equip, and maintain the necessary school buildings. Teachers must be hired and programs of study authorized. This is under the control of the school directors who are chosen by the town school meeting. Here, or at the Town Meeting itself, a Union High School District for several towns may be created by the required vote in the different towns.[29] Union Elementary School Districts may come into existence by the same route,[30] and all taxes for school costs can be appropriated and provision made for their expenditure.[31]

Originally, it was the custom in Vermont to hold the Town Meeting and the Town School District Meeting at different times. In recent years increasing use has been made of the practice of holding both meetings on the first Tuesday in March. This insures a larger attendance and a more rounded picture of the total town finances and town affairs. The warning for the school meeting must be as explicit as that for the town meeting. The statutes permit the selectmen alone to issue the warning which will be sufficient for both meetings,[32] but a common and wiser practice is to have the school directors also affix their names to the warning. This is legally unnecessary, but leaves less chance for misunderstandings to arise, and also represents a degree of cooperation which is valuable. As for the school meeting itself, common practice provides for a recess in Town Meeting, the convening of the Town School District Meeting, and the transaction of its business. This done, the Town School District Meeting is adjourned, the Town Meeting reconvenes, finishes up its last minute business and adjourns until the next annual or prior called meeting.

Since the citizens of a town are sovereign within the limits fixed by the laws of the state, it follows that they may vote upon almost

29   16 VSA   §   601 ff.
30   16 VSA   §§   571, 572.
31   16 VSA   §   3222.
32   16 VSA   §   362, Town school directors may not legally warn town school district meeting, 1956 Op. Atty. Gen. 108.

any item they wish, if they petition for its inclusion in the warning, or the selectmen wish to include it. Many items of interest are found in the several towns each year. Thus, the town may vote for the use of the Australian ballot, and just as easily vote it out again.[33] There can be a vote on a memorial for soldiers and sailors,[34] one for hospital construction or the use of hospital beds for care of the needy,[35] and a vote on the hiring of doctors by the town or in co-operation with other towns,[36] or a sharing in the costs for a visiting nurse.[37] There can even be a vote for funds to give the town outside publicity,[38] and action which has been taken for many years by the towns in the "Northeast Kingdom" in support of a regional program.

A town manager system can be voted in or out of the town government.[39] Public buildings can be constructed,[40] and a planning commission created when there is an article in the warning and the town so votes.[41] A zoning plan may be authorized.[42] Town fire districts can be created,[43] and the town can vote to own, maintain, and create cemeteries,[44] as well as to accept trust funds for their upkeep.[45] A building inspector may be chosen to stop improper construction and to forestall fire hazards by preventing the erection of poorly planned structures. The Town Meeting may decide to build lighting facilities for the roads and streets and to construct sewers and sidewalks.

In recent decades a new situation has confronted the towns-people — the necessity of considering the acceptance or rejection of grants and subsidies from the state. As towns have found it increasingly difficult to find the necessary revenues to meet the in-

33	24	VSA §	726.
34	24	VSA §§	3901 - 3903.
35	24	VSA §§	2601 - 2602.
36	24	VSA §	2604.
37	24	VSA §	2605.
38	24	VSA §	2743.
39	24	VSA §§	1231 - 1243.
40	24	VSA §	2802.
41	24	VSA §§	2901 - 2904.
42	24	VSA §	3002.
43	24	VSA §	2541.
44	18	VSA §§	5361, 5373.
45	18	VSA §	5383.

creasing demands of their citizens they have turned, or been forced to turn, to the state for assistance. In some instances the state has taken the initiative in an effort to help the towns to provide uniform levels of service. In any event, the towns have to raise enough revenue to match the proffered funds, and this often means a painful struggle before a decision can be reached. In a third of the Vermont towns these state payments constitute over fifty per cent of the total operating costs of local government. Towns are not the free agents they once were.

The above listing explains why so many of the citizens of the town stay home from the Town Meeting or wonder if it is all worth while when they do attend. They often feel that there are just too many technicalities of an administrative nature for them to study. Some of those who do participate wonder if it would not be better to combine several towns and have full-time employees to make the decisions, thus requiring only acceptance or rejection of the official program by the town.

A.   AN ILLUSTRATIVE EXAMPLE —

A TOWN MEETING DAY

Town Meeting day used to be the big event of the year, and even today still retains much of its former glamor. Spring is on the way, sap is beginning to run in the maple trees in the "sugar bush," and the long winter evenings have been productive of much thinking. It is pleasant to assemble before ten o'clock in the morning of the first Tuesday of March and chaff with one's friends and pass remarks about giving them a few headaches by putting them into office. But under all the good fellowship is the serious business of the day. A brief description of a portion of work and procedures of one of the 238 annual Town Meetings of some years ago, may illustrate both the strength and weakness of the Town Meeting.

This town had about 700 listed polls, or adult citizens. About nine-thirty in the morning the constable and tax collector took his position at the door leading into the main room of the Meeting House. As each person came along he was either admitted to the meeting, as having paid his poll tax before February first,[1] or was sent up to the balcony as a delinquent taxpayer, where he took his place along with the children, strangers, and others who could not vote.

In this particular meeting, no more than 110 voters were present at any one time. During the day an additional 90 or so voters came in to cast a ballot for or against the sale of intoxicating liquor, but these persons did not linger to participate further in the proceedings. Only two sevenths, or less than a third of the adult citizens of that town took part in the meeting of that day. It is the widespread nature of this abstinence from town affairs that causes many of the fears about the future of the town system of government.

The Town Report had been in circulation for some time and was a model of clarity, containing much material of informational value. The citizens who were present thus had had access to a good picture of the town's affairs. The moderator, chosen without opposition in the first item of business, was an old hand at the game and so business proceeded smoothly. Prior to the elections the town officers spoke briefly of the matters set forth in the Town Report, and the Report was accepted by the town. There was a real contest for the one selectman to be chosen, but there was no trouble and the office changed hands without further ado. The other officers were duly elected and received public acclaim.

Then came the important matter of deciding the tax rate for the coming year. After the first selectman had moved that the proposed budget be accepted, and the motion was duly seconded, there was the usual discussion about the need for economy. This budget had been worked out carefully by the selectmen and told of the town's past expenditures, the present year's costs, and the proposed future needs. One of the town die-hards, with a desire to embarrass the selectman, made an impassioned plea for a reduction in the proposed tax rate and asked that it be twenty cents less than the figure asked for. After making the motion, which was not seconded, he then sat down.

This was the signal for the first selectman to rise to his feet and ask everyone to turn to the budget as presented in the Town

---

1 Today the law has been changed and the date is January first. 24 VSA § 701.

Report. He explained that this was the story of what the town had done the preceding year; he asked them to review and evaluate these activities. The selectman then pointed out that the best judgment of the selectmen as to the work and need for the coming year was presented in the budget, and closed by saying that he was willing to cut the tax rate, but that he would like to know just which one of the proposed expenditures the town wished to reduce.

There was a nodding of heads all around the room, the die-hard blushed and one or two persons said that they thought the selectmen had done a good job. No further discussion arising, the moderator asked for a vote for the new tax rate and it was passed almost unanimously. The rest of the meeting passed off without incident, the voters present giving their consent to almost all the other items in the warning.

This Town Meeting gave abundant proof of advance work having been performed — the officers had prepared a clear account of their work, the auditors had approved, and the townspeople had studied the Report carefully. There was no lack of interest on the part of those present; they stayed throughout the day — the faithful one-seventh. There were no forensics, but a careful survey of business, and an intelligent discussion of the important issues. The stranger could not help but be impressed by the quality of this Town Meeting.

The moral of this illustration is the value of full information being available to the townspeople. Good work had been done throughout the year, the issues were understood, and every voter present felt that he had taken his part in reaching decisions. The general consensus was that with the increasing clarity and value of the Town Report interest had increased in recent years. Far from dying out, in this town the Town Meeting was growing in importance.[2]

There is no substitute for knowledge, and only an informed citizenry can make correct and valid judgments. What methods are available for gaining the necessary information, and what is the role of the town officers in the process? To these questions succeeding sections of this study will be directed.

---

2 Current observers in this same town report that this situation holds true in 1963.

SECTION II

Town Officers and Their Work

General Officers

The inhabitants of the first settlements in Massachusetts exercised the right of discussing and voting on local issues. As previously stated, it was not long until meeting once a week for the transaction of this local business became too much of a burden for the townsmen, and they began to choose a committee of varying numbers of men and empowered them to act in the place of the town in most "prudential matters." As it developed, this arrangement made it possible for the townspeople to remain inactive except for one meeting a year when they assembled for the annual Town Meeting.

When the first charters were granted by Benning Wentworth for land in what is now Vermont they required that meetings of the inhabitants and proprietors be held to conduct the same business and to choose the same kind of officers as was then the custom in New Hampshire.

CHAPTER 3

The Moderator

The statutes of Vermont provide that at each annual meeting
the town shall choose a moderator from among the legally qualified
voters of the town who shall serve until the next annual meeting
and until his successor is chosen.[1] It is the function of the moderator to preside at Town Meeting,[2] and to preserve order — he has
the privilege of ordering removed from the meeting any disturber
who refuses to quiet down.[3] There are no other Vermont laws pertaining to the moderator, and these bare bones of the statutes do
not convey a very complete picture of the officer in whose hands
the Town Meeting becomes either a smoothly functioning legislative body or an ineffective gathering of querulous individuals. Because of this, it is not surprising that many towns have found it ex-
pedient to re-elect the same man moderator for years on end.

The moderator must be a man of tact. He must know how
to turn away a harsh answer and how with a touch of humor to appear unperturbed by bitter comment. He must be able to permit the
mutterings of the town complainer to go on without offending
those who are anxious to get on with the town's affairs. In many
other ways the good moderator soothes and pacifies, and with it all
keeps himself and his ideas in the background. Any other course
of action destroys his value as a trusted, impartial, presiding officer.

Probably the most important function of the moderator is to
preserve parliamentary decorum. This means that all who are entitled to speak must be given the opportunity, that all questions

---

1 24 VSA § 711.
2 24 VSA § 724.
3 24 VSA § 725.

must be put to a vote when discussion comes to an end, and that
only those matters which are in order shall be taken up at any given
time. It is here that a good moderator comes into his own, for few
people are truly learned and up-to-date in Robert's Rules of Order
and similar handbooks. Yet, without following a few simple, generally accepted and regular rules no legislative action is possible.
It was once true that most of those at Town Meeting had attended
from boyhood and were able to carry on the old traditions. (Until
just prior to the 19th amendment to the federal Constitution women
were not allowed to participate.) But this is now no longer true.
New people from away move in, and many local residents appear
so infrequently that they have long since forgotten the procedures.
Sometimes the Town Meeting gets out of hand and becomes unruly
because no one, least of all the moderator, is able to trace a path
through the maze of conflicting motions, amendments, and shouts
which arise. Vainly the moderator calls for order and few hear him;
he has lost control because he failed to maintain his original advantage in controlling procedure and recognizing speakers.

As an illustration of how a good moderator can steer action,
one Town Meeting, attended by the writer will be mentioned. As
he looked over the gathering the moderator realized that there
were many persons present who had never before taken part in
a Town Meeting. Accordingly, just as soon as the meeting had been
called to order and the clerk chosen, he gave a fifteen minute talk
on the duties of the voters and the procedure to be followed. He
stated, first of all, that everyone who wished to speak on a matter
could do so, but that a second talk on any point could be made
only when no one else wished to speak for the first time. When the
discussion had gone the rounds it would then be possible for short
questions and answers to be bandied about.

Next, the moderator stated that when the meeting wished to
take action someone had to move that the matter be acted upon,
and that it then had to be seconded by someone else. Following the
second, anyone could speak but to that question only, or to
amendments made to the original motion. All amendments were
to be voted upon before the main motion was to be put, or voted
upon. The moderator briefly explained the method of voting on
amendments and their amendments and in this manner gave an
effective short course in paliamentary procedure.

Many persons squirmed and looked pained, for to them this was "old stuff," but the newcomers appeared grateful. The short time taken up in this explanation was time well spent, for it appeared that nearly all the voters present understood their rights and responsibilities. Several times during the day the moderator was asked to clarify some point so that the proper steps might be taken. The result was an harmonious meeting where everyone who so desired had a chance to speak, and at the day's end no one left saying that he had not been heard. Verbal sparks flew a good many times, but the votes taken were understood and came after proper consideration. It was reported to the writer that that Town Meeting transacted more business more speedily than was customary, and more people were satisfied with the votes.

It was at this same meeting that the moderator exemplified the first rule of a presiding officer, i.e., never participate in the debate while presiding. As a citizen of the town a moderator has the right to debate on any issue, but when he does so, parliamentary practice requires him to relinquish his post to another person called from the audience. He then goes to the floor of the meeting to state his views and to participate in the debate. When he has concluded his remarks, and perhaps, has voted on the issue, he again assumes his position. Almost every Vermonter who has attended town meetings can recall instances when this rule was not followed and the meeting became confused because the moderator took such a part in the debate that no one could tell when he was acting as presiding officer and when as a partisan citizen. A few moderators proceed in this highly questionable manner.

CHAPTER 4

The Town Clerk

Although the town clerk is the next official to be elected after the moderator, the sequence of the meeting would make it appear otherwise. In Vermont it is the custom for the clerk to open the Town Meeting at the prescribed hour of ten o'clock by calling the citizens to order and reading the warning for the meeting. This done, the clerk calls for nominations for moderator and sees that the vote is taken. He then turns the meeting over to the moderator. This action is taken despite the fact that the law states that the moderator is elected and holds office until his successor is elected.[4] It is custom and not law which has the town clerk open Town Meeting.

The newly elected moderator then calls for nominations for clerk. Ordinarily, there is but one name submitted and the election follows as a matter of course. At this point, in some towns, the clerk then reads the minutes of the last year's meeting, after which he begins the tedious task of recording the actions of the meeting. Frequently the moderator would be at a loss if he did not have recourse to the clerk's record of motions made, amendments proposed, and the votes taken on each item taken up. Thus it is that at every meeting the wise moderator should insist that the clerk record the exact words of the motion made, and its amendments, and then record the action taken as he has announced it. The clerk should insist that no questions be put by the moderator until the record is made accurately. Many needless town disputes and wasteful expenditures of money could have been avoided if this simple and necessary cooperation had been effected. In this situation the town clerk is carrying out one of the duties of his office. The chief function of the town clerk is the careful preservation of all the town

---

4 24 VSA § 711.

records.

It is not surprising then that ordinarily the town will re-elect the town clerk for just as many years as he or she wants the job and performs the duties satisfactorily. A recent, present day record, so far as the writer knows, was held by Mr. F. W. Kellogg, town clerk of Benson, who was first elected in 1898, and re-elected every year until his death in 1954. The late Mr. R. T. Robinson who was town clerk of Ferrisburg was the fifth in his family to hold the office, and upon his death his wife was elected to the post and served until her recent retirement and subsequent death. The Ferrisburg town records had been kept in that family home for over a century. In other towns the clerks have held office for equally long periods of time — a clerk in Craftsbury serving for sixty years. He was one of five clerks who had served the town from 1791 to 1938. A clerk in Warren served for fifty-four years.

Through the years the town clerk has become the officer who acts as the cement which binds the town structure together. Other officers may hold an office nearly as long, but they tend to be versed in but one aspect of the town's business. The town clerk has to know all the aspects, for the records of all officers are filed with him. When new officers are elected they come to the clerk who shows them where to turn for information, and then helps them learn how to use it.

The town clerk is the keeper of, and responsible for the preservation of the town records. These include all the official documents from the first parchment or leather charter granted to the first proprietors of the town, through the records of their meetings, and down to the minutes of the last Town Meeting. State law further provides that these records be kept in a safe place, not in an abandoned hen-coop, a damp basement, or a dusty attic. A recent law further provides that the records shall be kept in a fire-proof vault.[5] However, many short-sighted town meetings fail to provide funds for such a vault until after the inevitable fire strikes, and then it is too late. Incalculable damage has already been done to the early records of Vermont by this lack of foresight. Most town clerks regret this situation and do all they can to remedy it, and in recent years have been able to talk their towns into building the necessary fire-proof

---

5   24   VSA   §   1178.

vaults, so that today there are many more than would have been believed possible in the past. The present Director of Public Records, in Montpelier, Mr. Olney W. Hill, deserves great credit for his constant support of programs providing for better record keeping.

Any Vermonter who has not gone into the town clerk's office in his home town and asked to see the early records and questioned the clerk about their significance has missed part of his heritage. But all the population should not go to see him or her at the same time. The clerk is a busy person, and too crowded an office would stop official activity. A stranger coming into a town with the intent of tracing a family relationship or buying property inevitably finds that he will have to go to the town clerk to find out what he wishes to know. He soon discovers what all townspeople already know; the town clerk is indispensable in the proper functioning of the town.

In addition to keeping the records straight and up-to-date the town clerk has many other duties which are prescribed by law.[6] Election notices have to be recorded and ballot boxes made ready. Election returns have to be recorded and sent to the proper state and county officials. Deeds must be recorded, mortgages and their releases must be copied, and certified copies of many different kinds of documents have to be made upon request and with the payment of the required statutory fees. Marriage licenses must be issued, but only after the clerk has satisfied himself that the preliminary legal requirements have been fulfilled by both parties. Births must be recorded, and deaths have to be recorded and the documents placed in the files, while burial permits have to be issued. In the recent past the clerks had a great deal of extra work as they made records of the documents and papers of returning veterans, so that they would be on file for future reference. Hunting and fishing licenses are issued by the clerk, as well as the annual dog licenses required by all towns.[8] Each failure on the part of the clerk to do his duty may be

---

6 See 24 VSA §§ 1151-1178, for a rather clear expression of these duties. One would also have to look through the other eight volumes of the statutes as well to find all references to the work of the clerk.

7 18 VSA §§ 5131-5143.

8 10 VSA § 4254 (No. 119 of the *Acts of 1961*), and 20 VSA § 3581.

punishable by a fine.[9]

The listers file their schedules with the clerk and a copy of their appraisals is made for the archives, and the benefit of their successors. Questions of previous valuation must be settled by referring to the schedules in the clerk's office, and he has to know just where to find the information. In many cases the clerk is elected town treasurer and keeps the books for the town's finances. Whether or not he serves in this capacity, he must assist the auditors in gathering and arranging the data upon which they base their report. This assistance usually makes it possible for the auditors to make the complete and accurate study which is required of them by law.

Every session of the legislature sees some new duty imposed upon the clerk, and some new task which changing times makes imperative. Each duty ordinarily carries with it some fee which the clerk uses to compensate himself for his time and work, and each new fee makes it necessary for him to explain why it must be charged. The town may vote to pay an adequate salary to the clerk, and then keep the fees the clerk receives as a part of the town funds. Or, the town may vote a small token salary, and then permit the clerk to keep the fees he collects to supplement the small salary allowed. But whatever the method of payment, the town clerk never gets what he is actually worth to the town. The office of the town clerk is the high peak from which to watch the functioning of local self-government, and few clerks who once get bitten by the office willingly relinquish it.

---

9 24 VSA § 902. This section applies to all other officers as well. The fine is $100.

CHAPTER 5

The Selectmen

Today, following old customs and the statutes based upon them, every town in Vermont has at least three selectmen who "shall have the general supervision of the affairs of the town and shall cause to be performed all duties required of towns and town school districts not committed by law to the care of any particular officer."[10] This brief statement implies far more than a casual reading would indicate since a monograph could be written about this office. A sizeable volume has been issued which contains nothing except the sections of the law which pertain to selectmen and their duties.[11] Annotations and interpretations to the materials in this *Handbook* would provide an unmanageable tome. Consequently, the following cursory discussion of the selectmen and their duties is presented as a mere introduction to the field.

Since the term of office for each member of the board of selectmen is three years, one selectman only is chosen, by ballot, at each annual town meeting for the three year term. If the town so wishes it may also vote for one or two additional selectmen for a term of a single year.[12] Before the newly elected selectman may legally perform any duties he must be sworn into office by the board of civil authority or by a justice of the peace and a record of the action must be filed with the town clerk.[13] When this has been done the board of selectmen is required to begin the year's work, which is to meet immediately and organize. They are required to choose a

---

10   24   VSA   §   872.
11   *A Handbook for Vermont Selectmen* by Paul Dunham and Claribel Morton, 1962, Government Research Center, University of Vermont.
12   24   VSA   §   714.
13   24   VSA   §   831.

chairman, who is usually the one in his third year of office, and, if they so vote, a clerk.[14] Generally the chairman is known also as the first selectman. The actions taken by the board must be recorded with the town clerk.

The selectmen are then required to appoint from the qualified voters of the town, three fence viewers; a pound keeper for each pound in the town; one or more inspectors of lumber, shingles and wood; one or more weighers of coal; and, a tree warden.[15] These appointive officials will all be discussed at a later point in this volume.

If the town has so voted, the selectmen must appoint one or more road commissioners. On the other hand, the Town Meeting may elect the road commissioner.[16] This officer has certain tasks pertaining to highways that are delegated to him by the law, and the selectmen are held responsible for seeing that their appointee performs his duties satisfactorily. If he is negligent, or fails to do good work, the selectmen may remove him from office after a hearing.[17] By a series of legal requirements the selectmen are responsible for a large portion of the road work of a town which is withheld from the control of the road commissioner, a situation which complicates the work of the selectmen. This will be discussed later on when highways are under scrutiny.

Unless the town votes separately for an overseer of the poor the selectmen must appoint this officer, or serve in this capacity as a body, or through one of their members.[18] In any case, the selectmen are responsible for the actions of the overseer, or for their own,[19] if they are serving in this capacity.

If the town has voted to pay the town officers for their services, [20] but has not stipulated the exact amount, the selectmen must make this decision, except in the case of their own salaries. If the latter amount has not been set by town vote the salaries or payments are fixed by the town auditors at the time of the annual

---

14 24 VSA § 871.
15 24 VSA § 871.
16 24 VSA § 711.
17 24 VSA § 716.
18 24 VSA § 711 (6).
19 24 VSA § 873.
20 24 VSA § 932.

audit.[21]

The selectmen have the responsibility for arranging for, and the acceptance of, the bonds of the town clerk, the overseer of the poor, the treasurer, the road commissioner, the school directors, the constable, the tax collector, and any other officers who handle town money.[22] The selectmen must pre-audit, and if they wish to do so, approve bills against the town and issue the necessary orders for the payment of the same.[23] They must also be alert to prevent any duplicate office holding for positions which are by statute said to be incompatible offices, i.e., town treasurer, auditors.[24]

The selectmen, the town clerk, and the justices of the peace in the town act as a board of civil authority[25] to count ballots,[26] and to perform certain other tasks such as that of swearing into office those who are not officially installed without this act.[27] The same group with the listers and the town treasurer, serve as the board for the abatement of taxes,[28] while the board of civil authority alone is to hear appeals for revision of appraisals and poll tax listing.[29] In each case all decisions made in fulfilling these duties must be recorded and placed on file with the town clerk.

Every even year the selectmen have to insert an article in the warning for the Town Meeting asking the town to vote on requesting the state auditor to send someone to audit the town books. If the vote is affirmative the selectmen have to see that this is done.[30] They are also required to build and maintain a monument to soldiers and sailors, or to lay out a town park, if the voters so request in the legal form by voting.[31] The selectmen may lay out water systems,[32] build and maintain adqueducts,[33] and perform many other similar

21   24   VSA   §   933.
22   24   VSA   §   832.
23   24   VSA   §   934.
24   24   VSA   §   737.
25   24   VSA   §   801.
26   24   VSA   §   720.
27   24   VSA   §   831.
28   24   VSA   §   1533.
29   32   VSA   §§   4405-09.
30   24   VSA   §   1962.
31   24   VSA   §   3901.
32   24   VSA   §§   3301-3316.
33   24   VSA   §   2801.

functions. If the town votes to use a town manager system the selectmen must make the choice of the proper man for the job and act
as the supervisory or policy forming agency for the town. The manager is responsible to the selectmen for his work and may be removed by them.[34]

This enumeration of the duties of the selectmen is only a
partial one, but it is sufficient to show the complexity of their tasks
as the chief policy forming agency in the town, subordinate only
to the Town Meeting. It is only fair to state that a large part of this
required work is performed almost without pay and frequently the
selectmen receive not even expense money for their outlay of time
and money in performing the town's business. The ordinary citizen,
wishing to lend a hand toward better government might well begin
by a careful choice of his next selectman.

A. THE SELECTMEN AND THE GENERAL FUND

In the preceding discussion there was a brief survey of the
many tasks which the selectmen of a town must perform, while
casual reference only was made to town finance. It is now necessary to discuss the General Fund, which is the town money for which
the selectmen are directly responsible and for which they must account.

Each year the selectmen must estimate their own proposed expenditures for the coming year, and add to this amount the sums
proposed for the town school district, the town highways, and other
special items required by law. The total figures are then translated into a tax rate of so many cents (or per cent) on the grand list. These
estimates are published in the auditor's annual report of town finances, for the public to see and to study.[35] (There will be later comments on the grand list and on the budget for which see pages 48-
50, 75-77). At the annual Town Meeting the voters, sitting as the
town legislature, vote for a tax rate which they believe to be right,
and may or may not be sufficient to meet the outlays proposed by
the selectmen and other officers. Upon the proceeds of this legally
voted tax rate the town must depend for its locally raised finances.

---

34 24 VSA §§ 1231 - 1243.
35 24 VSA §§ 1681, 183.

The tax rate voted by the town is usually the sum of the several parts noted above, although some of these parts are for special purposes and funds and must be kept separate from the rest of the money raised. Among these special funds are those collected for schools and for highways.[36] Together with the amount collected for Old Age Assistance through the poll tax, less fifty cents remaining in the town for each poll, the total amount for these funds must be turned over to the proper officers.[37] If there is any deficiency or tax delinquency, the total amount not collected is to be deducted in its entirety from the money available to the selectmen in the general fund.[38] Thus, the special services receive the full amount of the tax levy, but the general work of the town must suffer or the selectmen go into debt to carry on the town's work when taxes are not paid in full.

One other matter also tends to reduce the amount of money available for the use of the selectmen. Many towns allow a discount of four per cent if the taxes are paid on or before a certain day,[39] and of those persons who intend to pay their taxes in any given year a goodly number take advantage of this discount. Unfortunately, the selectmen and the voters may have considered only the total amount needed and have made no allowance for the discount. Under this arrangement, even if all the taxes are paid the town will be a minimum of four per cent short of its total needs.

However, because of some tax delinquency there is seldom full payment, and the town actually receives much less than 96 per cent of the money it needs. When this occurs it is the selectmen's general fund that has to bear the full brunt of the losses, for, as stated above, the total amount of the levy voted for the special funds must be turned over to those accounts. There is no allowance for discount here. To take care of this situation, the town that wishes to give a four per cent discount on taxes paid on time should plan on raising, through the tax rate voted, at least 110 per cent of the amount it plans to spend. This is all the more imperative because the costs of collecting all the tax money raised is borne by the

---

36 32 VSA §   4791.
37 For schools see 16 VSA §§ 3262 - 3266.
38 24 VSA §   1526.
39 32 VSA §   4773.

general fund. If the town will so vote, the task of the selectmen in balancing the budget will be simplified greatly.

The statutes state that if there is a deficit in the operating expenses of the town in any year, the selectmen shall, in units of five per cent or multiples of five per cent, add to the tax rate voted by the town for the ensuing year enough income to make up the deficit.[40] If, through the neglect of the selectmen, or the refusal of the town to vote sufficient funds, some arrangement is not made for getting out of debt, the operating deficit soon becomes a part of the bonded debt of the town through consolidation of its debts. This is a short-sighted and poor business policy, and can only result in eventual bankruptcy. Since the statutes also restrict legal indebtedness to a figure equal to ten times the grand list,[41] continuing operating deficits will result in grave handicaps when there is need for capital public improvements.

In addition to this matter of insufficient funds the selectmen have other problems. If, for instance, the highway commissioner overspends his budget, he so informs the selectmen who must thereupon take over the control of the highways and see that the necessary work is done. This might well drain funds from the general fund which the selectmen had intended to use for other necessary expenditures.[42]

However, there are ways in which the general fund may be kept liquid. One method is through careful budgeting, something sadly neglected in Vermont, or if attempted, not completed. Later on in this study the matter of budgeting will be discussed at greater length. (See pages 75-77.) Another method would be to end the discounts for on-time prior payments of taxes, as stated above, and instead vote the legal one-half of one per cent per month penalty for non-payment of remaining balances on time as is authorized by the legislature.[43] Or, if it is desired to keep the discount, it is imperative that the town vote the suggested added tax which will give it the full amount of money needed to finance its activities. Still another method would be for the town to vote, year after year,

---

40 24 VSA § 1523.
41 24 VSA § 1759.
42 19 VSA § 101.
43 32 VSA § 5136.

a bigger tax rate than is needed to clear all anticipated needs. This would provide a surplus for emergencies and for preventing financial difficulties. Such a practice would be unwise without a very carefully worked out budget and full citizen support and understanding of the program.

The general fund is often the key to fiscal success in town government. Some towns have mastered its problems and are today wholly out of debt, and even have the small surplus suggested to take care of unforseen contingencies. This success in fiscal activity means that the town has formulated a program of planning for future town needs in a manner which has gained popular support because its implications were understood.

Financial Officers and Town Finances

CHAPTER 6

The Listers

Throughout the history of mankind the organization known as government has required financial support for its activities and for payment of its officials; the individuals who have lived under governmental protection and control have had to pay for the privilege. So much has this been the case that one of the most common folk sayings is, "Only two things in life are certain — death and taxes." The elementary truth inherent in the saying will, in all likelihood, continue. Since, then, taxation is an inevitable part of civilization, some reasonably fair and just method of distributing the burden of payments must be found. This is particularly necessary where people govern themselves, because there is no force applied to them except that authorized through their own actions.

In all the years since Vermont was first settled, the general property tax has appeared to its citizens to have this characteristic of fairness and justice, and consequently, has been the chief source of revenue for the towns, and for the state as well until 1931, when a state income tax was substituted as the chief source of revenue for the state. This same pattern of a gradual change from the general property tax to other sources of revenue for the upper levels of government has been followed in all except a few of the most backward states in the Union, so that Vermont is not unique. Uniformly, the general property tax has been left in the hands of the local governments, and it is now necessary to discuss its use in the towns of Vermont.

The general property tax is one levied upon real estate, i.e., land and buildings, and upon personal property, i.e., items like

37

jewelry, money, stocks and bonds, furniture, stocks of goods, and livestock. The first three items of personal property are called intangibles because they can so easily be hidden from the tax officials and thus escape the tax levies, and all others are called tangibles. Before any tax can be levied fairly upon any property it is necessary to find the value of the separate items belonging to each owner so that his proportionate share of the local taxes may be assessed against him.

In the towns of Vermont the duty of determining the value of property for tax purposes falls upon elected officials who are called listers, instead of the more familiar term assessor which ordinarily is used in most states. The term lister goes back to the early days of Vermont and was based upon the requirement for these officers to take the "list" of property owned by individuals. The current laws all reflect this in their use of the word *list* in the term "the grand list," etc. There is a board of three listers in each town, with staggered three-year terms of office. One lister is elected at each Town Meeting, except when death or resignation requires a vacancy to be filled for the one or two years remaining in the term of the ex-officer. These officers, as is so often the case in Vermont, are usually re-elected for term after term — the writer knew one person who had held the post for twelve terms.

The citizens direct more criticism at the listers and their work than at any other town officials except, perhaps, the selectmen. It is the lister's misfortune that his duties pinch and impress the pocketbook nerve of the voters. Until recently, the listers were expected to work only a few days per year, except during the quadrennial, for a fee of perhaps less than $100 per year. They were untrained amateurs who had to learn their job as they did the work.

The work of the listers is outlined very carefully in the Vermont statutes, as it has been from the enactment of the first existing laws of Vermont. These early laws carefully stated the exact valuation of each article: horse, sheep, watch, or furniture,[1] and, in addition, for many years included a "faculty tax" for professional peo-

---

1 *Acts and Laws, Passed by the General Assembly of the Representatives of the Freemen of the State of Vermont at their Session at Bennington, February 11th*, A.D. 1779, pp. 8-11. Hereafter this publication will be cited as *Laws of 1779*.

ple,[2] almost a forerunner of our modern income tax since it was based upon the estimated earnings of each person. Eventually these exact listings of values were abolished and the listers were required to exercise their own judgment as to the true value of the property.[3] From 1825 until recently, the form of the laws had remained essentially the same.

Up until 1957, Vermont had this ancient system of appraising property. The listers found the value of personal property every year, but the value of real estate was set every four years in the "Quadrennial Appraisal." Nominally, this meant that every parcel of real estate was to be "viewed" each fourth year on all its boundaries by the listers, and after this had been done, the appraisal value was to be determined by the board of listers. In practice, most listers merely drove over the roads of the towns, looked at the property as they went by, and then copied the figures from the last grand list book into the new one. Or, sometimes they merely sat in the town clerk's office and copied the old figures into the new book, determining any changes they thought necessary as they chatted and gossiped about the doings in the town. The only times when changes of importance were made was when a fire had destroyed the buildings on a parcel of land and they had not been replaced, or when additional value could be given to new buildings upon the land. Changes of this nature could be made yearly, but the basic value of the land could not be changed except at the four year interval. Because there was little or no reflection in the grand lists of altered conditions and times, there was a great deal of complaint, and, in consequence, there were many proposals for change. The combination of pressures finally bore fruit when, in 1957, the legislature abolished the "Quadrennial" in all towns by 1961, and permitted those towns, who wished to so vote in Town Meeting, to abolish it before that date.[4] The listers may now change valuations of real estate any and every year when it is necessary and proper. This has augmented the problems of the listers who may not have the time available or the ability to do the work called for.

Under existing statutes the work of the listers is based upon the

2 *Ibid*, p. 11.
3 No. 9 of the *Laws of 1825*, pp. 10 - 12.
4 No. 219 of the *Acts of 1957*, pp. 184-185.

date April 1, each year, for the law says that they are to fix the value of all property as of that date. Destruction or loss of property later on in the year does not exempt the property holder from paying taxes on non-existent property, because he had it in his possession on April 1. The valuations are placed upon both real and personal property. Each spring, sometime before April 1, the Commissioner of Taxes in Montpelier is required to furnish the listers of Vermont with blank forms known as "inventories."[5] On these forms are certain interrogatories and spaces for listing the property of the taxpayer. These inventories are to be used by the lister in determining the personal property holdings of the citizens, and to list the real estate and its owners as it was on April 1, in the given year.[6] In the smaller towns the listers hand out the inventories to the citizens, while in the larger cities and towns the ordinary citizen never sees the document and never pays taxes on most of his personal property. Failure to be given the inventory, where this is the practice, does not excuse the taxpayer from the obligation to get one or to be liable for taxes on the property. The taxpayers' inventories must be notarized and false statements are subject to the penalties of perjury. If the taxpayer refuses to fill out an inventory or the listers feel that he has made deliberate misstatements, or the taxpayer refuses to permit the listers to view his property, the listers may set down any figure which they feel to be a reasonable one, and it is up to the taxpayer to refute the figures of valuation. Otherwise, the taxpayer is liable for the taxes levied on the basis of the listers' figures, which often-times are understandably higher than might otherwise be the case.[7]

Personal property may be hidden with relative ease, and there are so many ways of claiming exemptions that Vermont, as is true in other states, does not get the tax money from this source that it should. There is much criticism against this portion of the tax burden and there are many persons who are vociferous in their demands that it be eliminated. Ordinarily, they make no realistic proposals for a substitute source of income, a matter of some import since the tax in 1963 approximated four million dollars.[8]

5   32   VSA   §   4001.
6   32   VSA   §§   3691, & 4004.
7   32   VSA   §   4084.

"Viewing" all the real estate is difficult and frequently the listers do not finish their work until well into the fall. They are not to be blamed for this delay, nor for a failure to find more property. They are usually part-time employees of the town who receive a mere pittance in money and much public opprobrium for their hours of work. The laws are causative of many delays.[9] Another major problem has been to find the property. Because of inadequate maps and even of surveying errors, there are some areas where many acres of land have been untaxed for years, or perhaps never taxed. The failure of the listers to view the boundaries of the land has prevented discrepancies from coming to light. Recently the state has authorized a complete aerial survey of the state, and very shortly every town can procure protographs from which accurate tax maps can be made. This will remove the excuse the listers have had for not doing what they have never done — listing *all* the real property in their towns. The complete listing may well decrease the tax burdens of those who have been paying full property tax by transferring some to those who have never paid their fair share.

Formerly the law said that real estate was to be set down at its true value in money,[10] which by common consent was interpreted as the price received for the property at an open sale where neither buyer nor seller was under any compulsion. This section was honored more in the breach than in compliance, and there was every variation in the valuation of property from a few per cent to over one hundred per cent. This was true not only for individual pieces of property, but for the average value of all property in a town in comparison with other towns. The result was chaos in the taxation picture. The situation was compounded in that every lister was required to sign an oath certifying that he would appraise all property at the figure (full value) required by law.[11] The Commissioner of Taxes used to say that every lister in Vermont perjured himself every year, and to correct the situation the Commissioner proposed legislation

---

8 Just this situation was presented during the 1963 session of the General Assembly when the bill to abolish the personal property tax was defeated.

9 32 VSA §§ 4341, and 4342.

10 *Vermont Statutes, Revision of 1947.* Sec. 748.

11 *Ibid.* Sec. 729.

which would make "honest men" of these officers. His repeated requests, plus pressure from the Vermont Listers' Association, resulted in the enactment in 1957, of a new oath which permitted the listers to find the "estimated fair market value" of property and to call this value the "appraisal value" of the parcel in question. The "listed value" of these items was to be determined by the lister as as proportionate part of the "appraisal value," and this fixed percentage, which was to apply to all property in the town, was to be recorded in the office of the town clerk. This percentage was to govern until the next year or until there was a new percentage fixed after some future listing period.[12] The significance of the "listed value" figure is that it is the basis of the town's grand list, a term which will be explained in subsequent pages.

An explanation for the earlier methods of appraisal lay in the attempt to create a low valuation for the townspeople's property, and this was felt to be a good thing for the town, largely because most of the population did not fully understand the harmful consequences of such action. In any given year it takes a specific amount of money to furnish the necessary funds to pay for the town's activities, and this money comes, in the first instance, from local taxes. If the valuation of property is low, the tax rate will have to be high, while if the valuation is higher the tax rate can be lower. The operation of this principle is demonstrated dramatically when a town or city has a complete and accurate appraisal made by an outside firm or by an energetic local board. The lower tax rate reflects the change in the value structure at once. Placing a true and accurate valuation on all property results in fairer treatment for all taxpayers; low valuations were usually fixed in a manner that permitted grave inequalities for many, and gave special and real benefits to a few persons.

Another explanation for underassessment was the state-grant-in-aid money to the towns which was based upon the grand lists of those towns. In general, the smaller the grand list the larger the proportionate payments by the state. Around 1940, there were approximately twenty programs for which state assistance could be received and, with this method of payment the accepted practice, it is

---

12   No, 239 of the *Acts of 1957*, p. 216, No. 175 of the *Acts of 1959*, p. 179, and 32 VSA § 3431, & 4381.

no wonder that the towns used competitive underassessment. The state thus acquiesed in illegal, or at best, questionable practices and placed a premium on their use. Recognition of the essential inequalities of this basis of payment finally came to the legislature, causing it to change nearly all the grant-in-aid laws by removing any reference to the grand list, except with respect to schools where larger state payments were made if the town increased its school tax in inverse proportion to its grand list. Although the bulk of these changes are now over twenty years old, some towns still act as they did when competitive underassessment was a benefit to them.

The basis of all property taxation should be consistent fairness to all and this may be achieved only through equalization of the grand lists. This means the same ratio of valuation of properties within a given town and the same ratio of valuation from town to town. When the townsman criticises the tax rate of his town it is not necessarily because he thinks it is too high, but often because he feels that neither he nor his fellow citizens are paying a fair and proportionate share in respect to other parcels of property. In fact, he can usually cite specific examples to show unfairness. It seems to the writer that one of the first steps toward equalizing the grand lists would be for each town to publish the statement of every person's list, either in the town report or in a separate publication. This is now done in some towns and seems to be beneficial; the townspeople can compare the legal valuation of their own property with that of their neighbors and see if the ratios are the same for everyone. It is said by some that this is a form of snooping and makes for trouble. The writer thinks that this is a weak argument. The best way to prevent rumors concerning property values and their unpleasant consequences is to present all the facts openly. In a free government everyone is entitled to the same treatment and this is not the case when there is no way to discover the real facts.

In an effort to find out just what is the actual tax base of Vermont the legislature in its 1963 session provided nearly $200,000 for a complete study of the value of all property in the state. The Tax Department was commissioned to make preparation for the study. It chose a group of six supervisors and twenty-four appraisers from a long list of applicants and suggested persons from the listers of Vermont. These thirty persons were given two weeks of intensive training and they then began at once the six months of work which was to embrace every town in the state and to involve every lister in one way or another.

This crash program is expected to be completed in early 1964, and it is hoped that for the first time the state will have a complete and accurate picture of general property taxes as a basis for support of local government. The program will also help to change the usual complaint that "Taxes just have to be reduced because we can't afford them," to a more modern statement "How can we get the most services at the lowest cost consistent with today's needs?"

A fact which is most often forgotten by people as they pay their tax bills is that the mutual sharing of governmental costs through taxation gives them far more for their money than they could purchase by their own efforts. How many people could afford to build a road or build, equip, and maintain a school? Yet by mutual cooperation all persons benefit at a relatively low cost per person for each service. An interesting fact here is that when people buy homes, automobiles, clothing, food, etc., they try to get the best quality they can afford, because they know that it will be cheaper in the long run. Yet, when they are buying governmental services they try to shop around for cut-rate programs. When services are purchased at the cost of unfair appraisals and too low tax rates, operating deficits pile up and there is great grumbling. Eventually the town must bond to get itself out of the financial doldrums and there is added cost for interest; the financial burdens of this unnecessary bonding often lead to still further attempts to get bargain rate sewers, water systems, and other enterprises with all the inherent dangers of improper construction and cheapness of materials which comes from the desire to "save" money. Statistics and common sense show that there are no bargain-counter public services. Community losses are so high when this approach is attempted that they are difficult to measure. Fairness and equality in taxation is a matter of continuously working for both — there are no short cuts.

HELPS FOR LISTERS

From the preceding pages the reader may have assumed that the nearly 750 listers in Vermont are on their own in carrying out their prescribed duties. This impression is erroneous because new aids have arisen and these aids have paralleled needs forseen by the writer in 1947 when he wrote:

"It seems to the writer that the next step is to see that a division be created in the office of the State Tax Commissioner where help would be available for the listers. One or more persons should be authorized to devote their entire time to this.

"These state helpers would have no power to coerce the listers, but would be ready to give suggestions when asked, and would have facts valuable to a hard-working lister. To get this information the state helpers would be authorized to go into the towns and make an independent valuation of several sample properties. When, in company with the local listers, they had found the full, reasonable valuation according to the best methods available, they would compare the new figures with those previously arrived at by the local officers.

"The comparison of the figures used by the listers and the men from the Tax Commissioner's office would undoubtedly show some variations. These variations could be used to determine what proportion of the fair value was the average value used by the listers in the town in question. This comparison of fair and reasonable values could be used by the listers as an aid for their own work, if they so desired. . . .

"As these comparative figures for the towns continued to accumulate in the State Tax Commission office year by year it would soon be possible for a town to compare its listing with any other town in the state. Since all the figures would be uniformly made they would serve as a valid check on property valuation for all concerned.

"The figures would be very valuable to the listers and would save them many headaches. When an angry property owner came to protest his listing it would be very helpful for the listers to be able to show the figures of an outside agency that would either back up the figures presented by the listers or show that they were giving the owner a great advantage by not using as high a valuation as should be used."

Although when these proposals were made they seemed to be mere day-dreaming, it is necessary to point out that almost this exact procedure has been followed by the office of the commissioner of taxes. There is now a division in that office, headed by a director of Local Property Taxes, which gives the kind of assistance called for.

The statutes have long provided that the listers shall be subject to the oversight, and advice, of the commissioner of taxes who provides many services for them, and who in turn expects cooperation from them.[13] In addition, the law permits the commissioner of taxes to employ special agents who have among their other duties the obligation to assist local listers in evaluating special classes of property.[14] In the few instances when special agents have been employed by the commissioner, the writer knows of none where their aid has been given to the listers.

The commissioner of taxes is instructed to call the listers together, either in groups or in a state-wide gathering, for purposes of training and instruction.[15] The listers are required to appear at any such meeting to which they are summoned in writing, and are entitled to a per diem stipend, and expenses for their trip, which are to be paid by their town.[16] For many years such training sessions were attended rather sparsely and resulted in but little tangible effect. About ten years ago the commissioner decided to hold a regular training school for listers at the University of Vermont. Ten sessions, each lasting for three or more days, have been held on the campus, while since 1961, an additional school of the same length has been held on the Castleton campus. In 1962, over a third of the listers in the state were in attendance. Only one lister from each town was "summoned." Some towns disregarded the summons while other towns sent the full board to participate.

Each year since 1946, there has been a Town Officers' Educational Conference, held first at Montpelier and then later at nine different places in the state. A total of 500 of the 738 listers in Vermont have been in attendance at one of the nine conferences in any one year. This one day session has been attended voluntarily and at the officer's own expense, except that recently, a few towns have begun to pay per diem and expenses.

The consequence of this concentrated effort to improve the work of the listers by teaching modern techniques by lecture and example has been a steady improvement in listing practices. Anyone who has followed the above-mentioned annual training programs has seen a year to year gain in understanding the work involved and in pride of accomplishment of the listers, many of whom

---

13 32 VSA §§ 3401 - 3406.
14 32 VSA § 3104.
15 32 VSA § 3434.
16 32 VSA § 3435.

proudly wear the five year button given for completing the three-day course five times. The desire of the officers to know their work better and the eagerness with which they accept the proffered assistance is an excellent example of the response citizens can make toward strengthening the democratic process. There are exceptions, of course, for among these offices as elsewhere there are those who know all the wrong answers and are determined to stand by the errors, come what may. "No one is going to tell me what to do."

CHAPTER 7

The Grand List

The specific function of listing property values is, however, only one stage in the fiscal activities of the town. Having established the valuation of property upon which local taxation is based, the next duty is to take the proper legal steps to translate all this work into tax receipts. Since local government costs are steadily rising, there is a greater and greater pressure upon the property owners which they are resisting as best they can. There are many who say that it is only a question of time until some other tax base must be found or there will be insufficient revenue to support local government. But as long as the general property tax is retained as a major source of local funds it is imperative that the true value of property be fixed in such a way as to retain and not kill off the sources. Here lie such questions as the revaluation of growing timber, idle quarries, and closed shops or plants. Unfair or too oppressive taxes could forever preclude the retention or reopening of these enterprises in towns that are already declining.

The basis of the tax levy for each person is his individual grand list. This grand list is made up of three series of figures. First, the listers put down one per cent of the total "listed value" of the real property which he owns. Second, they do the same for his taxable personal property.[17] Finally, a figure of one dollar, as one per cent of the legal value of a taxpayer's "body," is set down.[18] (Mention only is made here of the one hundred dollar value set for each taxpayer between the ages of twenty-one and seventy, except for certain veterans, and a restricted list of other persons.)[19] The sum of these

---

17   32   VSA   §   3482.
18   32   VSA   §   4152 (6).
19   32   VSA   §   3801. See also p. 51ff below.

48

figures is the basis for all subsequent action. Until 1947, this procedure was complicated by the requirement that there be an "offset" for debts owed, which was a figure subtracted from the valuation of the personal property of the debtor, after the "offset" figure had been derived from certain prescribed complicated computations. No one really objected to the demise of this offset law.[20]

The abstracts or summaries of each individual taxpayer's grand list, as derived from the inventories, are placed in the town Grand List Book which must be filed in the town clerk's office, after its correctness has been sworn to by the listers.[21] This town grand list is open for public inspection, but the individual inventories from which it is made are not available except to the owner himself, or to the proper town officials (listers, etc.,) certain other specified officials, and the courts.[22]

An abstract or summary of the town grand list must also be made by the listers, sworn to, and filed in the town clerk's office.[23] The town clerk must in turn verify its accuracy[24] and transmit a copy of the accurate or corrected document to the Commissioner of Taxes, as well as any subsequent corrections or additions which may be made.[25] The sum of the figures in the abstract of the town grand list is the basis used in figuring the town taxes, just as the abstract of the individual's grand list determines his share of the town taxes. Usually the procedure of fixing the tax rate follows a regular pattern. Prior to the Town Meeting each officer who spends money estimates his next year's needs and fixes the total amount of money required. This figure is given to the selectmen, or to the selectmen and budget committee in those few progressive towns that have a real budget, and the total of all the proposed expenditures is determined. The selectmen, with or without the listers' help, guess at the grand list figures for the next year. (The correct figures must eventually be substituted for this guess before the tax bills go out, and this sometimes causes problems because of the variation in the two sums.) This guessed amount is then divided into the total esti-

20   No. 13 of the *Acts of 1947*, p 26.
21   32   VSA   §§   4141, & 4152.
22   32   VSA   §   4009.
23   32   VSA   §   4181.
24   32   VSA   §   4183.
25   32   VSA   §   4185.

mated expenditure and the quotient thus found is the proposed tax rate for the ensuing year. It is spoken of as so many cents on the grand list, which really means per cent of the grand list. The total in the quotient may well be, for example, some such figure as 494 cents on the grand list, or a town rate of $4.94. In this total the proposed expenditures of the individual officers may vary from a few cents to one or more dollars.

The town school district uses the same procedure in arriving at the town school district tax rate. Their estimate is given to the selectmen who must add it to the proposed town tax rate. Usually in Vermont these totals now approximate an average rate of $10. The totals in this proposed complete town tax rate are presented at Town Meeting and the town may accept them as they are, reject them, or change any and all sections. The final figures are those voted, and represent the collectable tax rates for the ensuing year. This two-part total tax rate, town and school district, also fixes the basis for the town poll tax, which with a few exceptions is assessed against every adult between the ages of twenty-one and seventy, residing in the town on April 1.

CHAPTER 8

The Poll Tax In Vermont

It is a tribute to the grasp of realities shown by the early founders of Vermont that they provided for public taxation almost with the same breath that declared the new republic founded. The first constitution in 1779, provided that taxes could be levied only when there was a law specifically authorizing the action. It further stated that the taxation must be more beneficial to the welfare of the state than the use of money would be if it were not collected.[28] Taxation was to be uniform and for public purposes.

The earliest laws of Vermont made provision for the levying and collection of taxes from every adult male. Each town was given authority to vote a tax, or rate, in order to raise funds to pay the costs of authorized activity.[29] Listers had to be chosen and they in turn were to determine the value of the real estate and personal property in each town,[30] as well as to make a list of all male persons from 16 to 60 years of age ". . . . (Ministers of the Gospel, The President and Tutors of the College, annual School-masters, and Students of the College, until the Expiration of the Time for taking their second Degree, excepted), shall be set in the List, each Person at six pounds."[31] These lists of males were to be used for levying a poll tax. Through the years since 1779 revisions of the laws have changed the valuation for each adult, varying the sum from $20 to $100—the current rate being one dollar. or one per cent of $100.

---

28 *Constitution of 1777*, Chapter II, Section XXXVII.
29 *Laws of 1779*, pp 24-25.
30 *Ibid.*, pp 8-11.
31 *Ibid.*, p 10.

51

The laws just mentioned were deficient in terms of enforcement and on October 15, 1782 an act of the General Assembly said, ". . . That every inhabitant of this state except such as are or shall be by law exempted, shall contribute to public charges, and shall be compelled therto [sic] (if need be) by distress, to be levied and collected in such a manner as is or shall be by law provided."[32] This statement appeard in almost the same form in every volume of the laws of Vermont until about the middle of the 19th Century when it disappeared as a formal enactment.[33] However, the ideas of this early statute remain the basic principle of modern laws under which all poll taxes in Vermont are levied today. The theory is that, even if he owns no personal property or real estate, every adult should contribute some tax money if he is to vote on town expenditures. Accordingly, no person is permitted to vote in Town Meeting until he has paid his poll tax, unless he is one of those persons exempted from payment under the law, or has reached the age of seventy. The exceptions are for certain soldiers of past wars, disabled veterans, and really poor persons.[34]

The basis of the poll tax is the rate which is voted by the Town Meeting to pay for the town needs. Unless legally exempted, any person who lives in the town must pay an amount equal to the sum of the rates of the governmental units in which he is living. Thus, a man must pay as a poll tax the rate of his town, his village, and any other municipal corporation in the town from which he benefits. This may bring the total poll tax to the neighborhood of twelve to fourteen or more dollars in some less fortunate towns. In addition, the law prescribes that every person between 21 and 70 must pay an Old Age Assistance Tax of $5.00, unless legally exempt, of which the town retains fifty cents for the costs of collection and remits the balance to the state treasury. This is augmented in some towns by a special poll tax.

In 1962, thirty towns were levying a special poll tax for various purposes — schools, improvements, etc., — and it was five dollars or more in each instance. The special poll tax started out in the

---

32 *Laws of 1782*, p. 13.
33 See for instance *The Laws of Vermont, 1824*, Chapter XLIX, Sec. 1. p. 400.
34 32 VSA § 3801.

beginning as a "soak the poll taxpayer" type of thing and at first was sanctioned by legislative action specific in nature.[35] Later, the law became general in nature and non-payment of the special poll tax did not remove voting rights in Town Meeting and it is now a minor source of revenue in the towns using it. The General Assembly in 1963, gave authority for school districts to levy a special poll tax not to exceed $8.00 and which is to be assessed, collected, and paid into the school fund separately from all other poll taxes.[36] The poll tax has thus become a formidable tax in many towns; the total may well be twenty-five dollars.

The town may vote as to what day the poll taxes are due; it can also decide if there is to be a discount for payment on or before that due date.[37] The selectmen are responsible for assessing the poll tax on every rateable poll and for placing the tax bill, which they must make up, in the hands of the officer who, by vote of the town, shall collect the tax.[38] The bread-winner in a family is responsible for the payment of his and his spouse's poll tax.[39] If it is unpaid he is not to vote in Town Meeting or get a driver's license for operating a motor vehicle. When the taxpayer is delinquent the officer charged with collecting taxes may start an action against him before a justice of the peace.[40] If the justice finds that the charges against the taxpayer are valid he may place a lien against his wages which are in excess of $10.00 a week. The collection shall not exceed $2.00 a week until the tax and penalties are fully collected.[41] It must be admitted that, at least in larger communities in Vermont, laxity in record keeping permits a goodly number of resident to escape payment of the poll tax.

---

35   See, for example, No. 97 of the *Acts of 1961*, p. 454. The index of the recent issues of the biennial *Acts and Resolves of the General Assembly*, reveal how much time is spent by that body in these special acts for individual towns. Approval by the General Assembly of requests by towns for the imposition of a special poll tax is almost automatic.

36   No. 40 of the *Acts of 1963*, pp. 43-44, (Temporary Edition).

37   32   VSA   §§   4773, 4774.

38   24   VSA   §   1521,   and   32   VSA   §   5015.

39   32   VSA   §   5011.

40   32   VSA   §   5091.

41   32   VSA   §   5092.

Regardless of when the poll tax is due, if the citizen is to vote in the coming March meeting, it much be paid before January 1. There is no requirement for payment of a poll tax before a primary or a general election, and thus there is no intent to prevent the exercise of suffrage except in Town Meeting. There is no doubt that the very low property assessment and very high tax rate followed in some towns is planned deliberately in order to penalize those who own no real estate. Non-property owners can be forced to pay well for the privilege of voting in Town Meeting with no question being raised as to the fairness of the tax on the basis of a proportionate share of income received. More study needs to be given to the subject if the very excellent principle of full participation in tax payments by everyone is not to degenerate into a means of making sure that only the "right people" vote.

CHAPTER 9

The Treasurer

Although a town may have an excellent board of listers who perform their work well, the effectiveness of the fiscal policy of the town government will be determined by the amount of money that the town actually collects on the established tax base. It is this sum which determines what the town can do and can pay for. Assessment is thus only half of the picture; the other half being the collection of the taxes voted. Because of ambiguities in the law it will be necessary to discuss the treasurer and the tax collector in the same context, for when the statutes outline the work of tax collecting both are referred to indiscriminately.

The statutes provide that there shall be a tax collector in every town, and states that if the town so desires it may elect a specific official in the Town Meeting.[1]   Or, if the town so decides, the treasurer may be elected as tax collector, and is constantly referred to in the statutes in that capacity. The tax collector may be chosen to perform the duty of collecting delinquent taxes only, while in some towns he collects all types of taxes.[2] If the town does not choose a tax collector of any type, the first constable automatically takes over the duties of tax collector and turns over everything he collects to the treasurer.[3] Since there is no set rule in Vermont towns about the choice of the collector, the discussion of the post has to be in the light of each town's own practices.

Since it is the treasurer who must receive, and have custody

---

1 24 VSA § 711.
2 24 VSA § 1528.
3 24 VSA § 1529.

55

of the town taxes, and to whom the collector must report when the two offices are separate, this officer will be taken up first. The town treasurer is one of those officers who exercises what is known as "ministerial powers." In other words, he is required by law to perform certain functions, and he has no discretion as to whether or not he will do so. If he fails to perform these duties he may be removed; if he does act, he may not be held liable for doing what he is required to do, i.e., paying out money by vote of the town, such vote later being found invalid.[4] In this, he is quite different from the selectmen who have broad powers of discretion as to whether they need act or not, and who usually take full advantage of this privilege.

The town treasurer is elected by the Town Meeting for a one year term of office, or until his successor is chosen. As explained above, the town clerk is often elected treasurer as well, and when this is the case the clerk has the interesting task, immediately after Town Meeting, of certifying his own name to the state treasurer as the duly elected town treasurer and then signing his name as town clerk.[5] To confuse matters still further the clerk-treasurer may be chosen as the collector to receive all but delinquent taxes. When this is the case, the treasurer must issue tax warrants to himself as tax collector, report the results of work to himself, as treasurer, and record and certify all the transactions as town clerk. All this contact with town money requires that he be bonded for such amounts in his varying capacities as the selectmen shall determine to be correct.[6] As town treasurer, this versatile official is also treasurer of the town school district[7] and is required to keep records of and pay out school district funds in the same manner as is called for by law for town finances.[8] There must be a separate account for the school funds.

Twenty-five days before the annual town meeting the treasurer is required to settle his accounts for the year with the town auditors.[9] This means that he must have the records for all the

---

4   24   VSA   §   903.
5   24   VSA   §   1166.
6   24   VSA   §   822.
7   16   VSA   §   3223.
8   24   VSA   §   1571.
9   24   VSA   §   1681.

money received, and the warrants or orders for the money paid out.[10] When cash in hand is added these two sets of figures must balance. Five days before Town Meeting the auditors are to make a final check to see that all is in order.[11]

The treasurer acts with the listers and board of civil authority as the board for the abatement of town and town school district taxes.[12] When this board has made its decisions and sent a copy to the treasurer and the tax collector, [13] the tax collector has to make a record of the abatement on the tax warrants which he has in his control.

When the state treasurer or the county treasurer draws a warrant for the payment of taxes owed by the town to either of these units of government it is directed to the town treasurer who presents it to the selectmen. They in turn draw the warrants authorizing the treasurer to make the payment, which he then does. This is an illustration of a ministerial power — the treasurer has no discretion in the matter.[14]

If the town does not vote a date for the payment of town taxes, the treasurer is to fix a date for payment, which is to be at least thirty and not more than ninety days from the date of the notice to this effect. This notice is to be published and a copy sent to the taxpayers as well. This date is to apply for the discount if it has been voted.[15] Within a fixed time, twenty days, after a payment of taxes has become delinquent the treasurer is to make a list of the delinquents and turn it over to the collector.[16] For complying with this requirement and completing the task the treasurer receives five cents per name, which amount is added to the delinquent taxpayer's bill.[17] When the treasurer collects the taxes he receives one per cent of the amount collected as his fee.[18] This amount must be kept in mind when the proposed expenditures are presented, for there is au-

10 24 VSA §§ 1571-1576.
11 24 VSA § 1578.
12 24 VSA § 1533.
13 24 VSA § 1536.
14 32 VSA § 473, and 24 VSA § 135.
15 32 VSA § 4792.
16 32 VSA § 4793.
17 32 VSA § 1673.
18 32 VSA § 1672.

tomatic deduction in the total amount available.

Several other functions of the treasurer need to be mentioned, at least, even though they may affect only a part of the citizenry. He must act as custodian of the funds belonging to the cemeteries of the town, and is required to keep track of the investments made in their behalf, and of lots sold and the receipts thereof.[19] The treasurer receives the funds derived from the dog licenses issued in the town, and is required to pay them out on the proper order for the purposes described by the law.[20] When the town finds itself without money and has issued registered warrants to pay for sewers, or goods consumed, the treasurer is charged with the responsibility of posting the time and day when these outstanding obligations will be paid. This action is necessary because no further interest will be paid after this date. There are the usual requirements, found in Vermont law, of posting the notices in three places in the town and of advertising in the locally circulated papers for at least three weeks prior to their date of redemption.[21] When the town has voted to permit the sale of bonds for a legal purpose the treasurer and the selectmen must sign the bond forms before they may be issued.[22] He is required to keep a record of the bonds sold, and if they are registered, he must keep the register for inspection.[23] His is the responsibility for keeping all these matters in order. One last function is to list and keep in order all the deductions from the general fund caused by the abatement of taxes, by the discounts allowed, and by the collection fees which have been voted or otherwise allowed.[24]

All these activities are routine tasks and require an orderly mind and a patience for detail. In addition, the treasurer must be scrupulously honest. There should never be a whisper of his having paid out money illegally or without full proper authorization. It is to the credit of most town treasurers that there is seldom difficulty in this respect. It is possible to count on one's fingers the cases in the past quarter century where any of the 246 treasurers have betrayed their trust.

---

19 18 VSA §   5377.
20 20 VSA §§   3542, & 3543. — These are payments for livestock or birds killed by dogs.
21 24 VSA §   1582.
22 24 VSA §   1763.
23 24 VSA §§   1771 & 1781.
24 24 VSA §   1526.

CHAPTER 10

The Tax Collector and Tax Delinquency

Turning now from the office of treasurer-tax collector to that of tax collector alone we find some variations and changes. The laws state that there is a slight difference in the way duties are carried out, and this has to be kept in mind at all times.[25] The tax collector, when it is so voted, is specifically charged with the duty of collecting and paying over to the treasurer all the taxes called for in the warrants, or rate bills, which the selectmen must prepare and turn over to the collector.[26] Whenever a majority of the selectmen, in writing, require him to do so, he must pay to the treasurer all the tax money received to date, and "submit his tax book and list to the treasurer for inspection and computation." Failure to comply within ten days may lead to a fine of one hundred dollars.[27] Obviously, this section is seldom used since it would be of value only when something improper is suspected and that seldom occurs in Vermont. The regular annual settlement with the treasurer of the town must be made in full by February 1st. Failure to do so makes the collector ineligible for re-election for the coming year.[28]

For his work the collector may receive such fees, voted him by the town, which are "judged advantageous to the town and town school district." This concept dates to the first *Constitution of 1777*. In place of the fees the town may vote a straight salary. When this is done the collector must pay into the town treasury, at least once a month, all the payments and fees he received since the last

---

25 32 VSA §§ 4791 - 4793.
26 24 VSA §   1521.
27 24 VSA §   1531.
28 24 VSA §   1532.

accounting.[29].

Rather rigid requirements are placed upon the collector because of the town's need for operating income. Delinquent tax payments are detrimental to these needs. A tax collector who is willing to do his job and who receives reasonable support from the other town officers can reduce the problem of tax delinquency almost to the vanishing point. An example of this was Rutland Town where for years on end the rate of collection was around 98 per cent of the taxes levied. Other towns have achieved this record for one or two years at a time and all such programs should be commended. Instead, in many towns, delinquent taxes accumulate until large sums are owing to the town and this becomes a very serious matter. During the 1930's non-payment became so prevalent that many towns went heavily into debt, and some of the taxes went unpaid for years. Since unpaid taxes remain a first lien upon property for a period of up to fifteen years, it would have been possible during the lusher war and post-war years to have collected these back taxes.

Every town should have a program for collecting back taxes and paying off accumulated deficits. Not to do so smacks of bad management. It is true that certain personal property taxes probably can never be paid because of the real poverty of the owners. When this is the case these taxes should be abated, as the law permits, and not carried on the town books as assets, as too many towns have long made a practice of doing. To so carry fictitious amounts of money gives a false picture of the town's financial health.

The state commissioner of taxes is charged with the responsibility of giving help in the collection of delinquent taxes. He is to call meetings of tax collectors at his pleasure to give them necessary help and instruction.[30] When the commissioner summons the collectors in writing, all those who receive the summons are required to attend. If, for some reason, a person is unable to attend a specified session and so makes his excuse to the commissioner, the commissioner can tell him what other called meeting he must attend. The town is to pay the collector ten dollars per day and his

---

29 24 § 1530, & 32 VSA § 1674.
30 32 VSA § 5133.

necessary expenses.[31] In addition, every six months, or whenever asked to do so by the commissioner, the collector is to report the total amount of delinquent taxes he has collected and turned over to the treasurer.[32] After each Town Meeting the town clerk is required to inform the commissioner what action the town has taken for the collection of delinquent taxes.[33]

The work of the tax collector varies from town to town because the Town Meeting has the right to vote different days for collecting taxes. The meeting may vote for installment payments,[34] and for the payment of interest on delinquent taxes,[35] or some other arrangement desired by the townspeople. All these variations complicate the work and add to the difficulties of keeping the records straight. For instance, if a town votes to collect taxes by installments and also to charge interest on over-due payments, interest may be charged on any one non-payment of the series. The legal rate for this interest is one half of one per cent a month or six per cent a year.[36]

Towns also may vote to permit a discount, not to exceed four per cent, for payment on or before a given date.[37] It was stated earlier that this is a bad practice, for such discounts reduce the general fund for the selectmen, and often result in indebtedness. There should be no discounts for pre-paid taxes, but there should be substantial penalties for delinquent taxes. The tax collector should not have to be bothered with figuring discounts on every installment, particularly when the discounts are not helping the town treasury.

Under current statutes the treasurer or tax collector may take the legal steps necessary to collect taxes due at any time he thinks a taxpayer is about to abscond without payment of his levy.[38] The official also has the right to seize and sell such portion of real estate holdings as may be necessary to collect unpaid and due taxes.[39]

31	32	VSA	§	5134.
32	32	VSA	§	51.66.
33	32	VSA	§	5167.
34	32	VSA	§	4871.
35	32	VSA	§	4873.
36	32	VSA	§	4874.
37	32	VSA	§	4773.
38	32	VSA	§§	4796, & 4875.
39	32	VSA	§§	5061-5078.

The delinquent has the right to challenge the validity of the tax, but, if the tax is legal and he still does not pay up, he may lose his property. Such drastic steps are seldom used, but they are provided so that they may be available when needed. The better method for the collection is to make every attempt to use persuasion and to explain the need for prompt payment before taking formal action. Most of the people who fail to pay taxes on time do so merely because of neglect and not out of malice or ill-will. Many experienced tax collectors have said that when a man who owes taxes is given an advance warning of unpleasant consequences he can usually find the funds to pay up, but, if the obligation is permitted to drag on, there are always seemingly valid reasons for the non payment.

The legal fees allowed to tax collectors are not very remunerative,[40] which is probably one reason a tax collector permits many taxes to become delinquent, — there is so little to pay him for his trouble. The same factor is present in collection of delinquent taxes,[41] and probably explains why the collector is willing to allow tax delinquency to pile up until the fees amount to a large enough sum to make the bother of collection worthwhile.

The tax collector is personally liable for all the taxes he collects, and may be forced to pay them, or surrender his property, if the need arises.[42] He is protected, however, if he has collected taxes that should not have been collected because of a defective warrant given to him.[43] Probably few people know if a tax collector does not pay a state tax into the state treasury at the time stipulated in his warrant for the collection of the same, the sheriff of the county, by order of the state treasurer, can seize and sell the goods and chattels of any citizen of the delinquent town for the amount of the tax due. The citizen who is thus used may recover the payment for these goods or chattels from the town in a suit against it. He is also entitled to twelve per cent interest, but that does not recover his lost property.[44] While such action may never be taken against any given person, its possible use should be kept in mind whenever the num-

---

40   24   VSA   §   1530.
41   32   VSA   §   1674.
42   32   VSA   §§   4691-4700.
43   32   VSA   §§   4641, & 4642.
44   32   VSA   §   4735, & 4736.

ber of delinquent taxpayers in a town begins to increase and in consequence the funds to decline.

It is often argued that the more collectors there are the greater the chance that tax money slip through their fingers. This may be true. It also has been suggested that instead of many persons doing the same job there be only one tax collector for several towns, or even for an entire county, as is the case in many states. This proposal merits favorable consideration. Under this arrangement it would be possible to pay an adequate remuneration for the work done. Greater interest on the part of the collector could mean fewer delinquent taxes carried along, because the larger area would entail full time work. If these changes were made, all taxes collected could be credited to the proper town treasurers who would then handle their own funds as they now do. Any practice which simplifies the handling of tax money is an advantage.

CHAPTER 11

The Town Auditors

The levying and collection of town taxes, and the legal processes prescribed by law to provide towns with funds to carry on the tasks delegated to them, have been discussed in preceding chapters. Once the tax money is in the hands of the treasurer, town officers spend it as they carry out their duties. The goods and services are paid for by warrants or orders issued by the officers. These warrants direct the treasurer to make payment therefor, and the treasurer must be satisfied that the officers' orders are drawn legally.

There is a further step — someone must check and verify all these figures to determine whether funds have been properly and legally handled and this is the task which falls to the town auditors. Every town has a board of three auditors, one of whom is elected each year by ballot at the Town Meeting for a three year term.[1] Because it would not be fitting for an auditor to verify his own accounts he is permitted to hold none of a series of listed incompatible offices, nor may his spouse.[2] This restriction does not apply in towns with fewer than twenty-five legal voters, except that an auditor in such a town is not to audit his own accounts in any other office it may be necessary for him to hold.[3] The auditor's task is often a thankless one and consequently few persons care to serve.

The officers of the town must turn the records of their warrants and orders over to the auditors for verification at least twenty-five days before the Town Meeting. Also, before this date, the

1 24 VSA §§ 711, & 713.
2 24 VSA §   737.
3 24 VSA §   738.

64

auditors must meet and "examine and adjust the accounts of all town and school district officers and all other persons authorized by law to draw orders on the town treasurer."[4] Town auditors are required to study and report on the trust funds belonging to the town; to verify all outstanding bonds; and to check any interest bearing notes of the town. Each year the cemetery commissioners file their report with the auditors.[5] The printed Town Report contains the results of these studies and must be distributed to the legal voters of the town at least five days before Town Meeting[6] — a requirement not always met, much to the detriment of the town.

After a long period of time when the town fiscal year ended on January 31, the General Assembly of 1939 made it possible to end the fiscal year on December 31. By No. 63 of the *Acts of 1939,* the Town Meeting was authorized to vote to make the change; once taken, the action was to remain effective until there was a specific vote to rescind the decision and to the writer's knowledge this has never been done. Most of the towns have availed themselves of the terms of this act and, consequently, the town auditors have more time to perform their duties.[7]

As the business of the larger towns has increased their auditors have found the tasks increasingly complex, and have asked for help. Even in smaller towns the same trend has appeared. In some cases, persons have been elected auditors with no idea of the task they were to perform. Protests from such officials, and other factors, resulted in action by the legislature in 1937, when No. 55 of the *Acts of 1937,* superseded but did not repeal an older section. This act, now a part of the statutes, provides for a biennial vote calling for help from the State Auditor's office.[8] A favorable vote means that that office is informed of the request and the town is placed seratim on a list of towns requesting audit. When the work is done and the books of the town audited, the state officials turn their report over to the local auditors,[9] who incorporate it in their own reports to the town, for

---

4 24 VSA § 1681.
5 18 VSA §§ 5379, & 5380.
6 24 VSA § 1682.
7 24 VSA § 1683.
8 24 VSA § 1692.
9 24 VSA § 1693.

which they are responsible.[10] The state officials may recommend
the installation of a better accounting system, and a better form for
the Town Report.[11] For all this work the town is to pay the actual
cost of the audit,[12] which by practice has been made as reasonable
as possible. Although many towns have availed themselves of this
service, its actual operation often leaves much to be desired, because
the state report is written in technical accountant's terms which
mean little to the average lay reader. If the town auditors would
translate this state report into more popular terms instead of just
reprinting it as received, it would have much greater value, increased
even more if the state auditors would give continued unofficial help
to the town officers.

While it is true that there is very little illegal expenditure in the
towns of Vermont, it is always possible to spend money unwisely.
Although frequently the auditors have had to guess at the money
raised and spent, they have had the opportunity to question officers and to bring to light wasteful practices. However, no workman
can do his best without the proper tools for his tasks, and makeshift
equipment can cause delays, difficulties, and frustrations. The same
holds true for town officers. Waste often comes about because town
officials lack one of the most important financial tools — an effective, yet simple, accounting system.

The late Benjamin Gates, former State Auditor of Accounts,
used to have a great many stories to tell about the methods of account keeping that he had found in some towns in Vermont. He
told of finding town accounts on the backs of old envelopes, on
pieces of scratch paper, on paper sacks, and even of being told
that the accounts were kept in the head of the reponsible official.
The results of such practices, they cannot be called business methods, were chaos and disorder. Gates also said, shortly before his retirement, that in his considered judgment nearly sixty-five per cent
of the towns in Vermont were then in some financial difficulty. He
was quick to add that he did not mean illegal keeping of money or
malfeasance in office, but that he was talking of sheer carelessness
that caused loss of needed money and made town costs too high.

---

10   24   VSA   §   1691.
11   24   VSA   §   1696.
12   24   VSA   §   1694.

Some years ago the writer read a survey of town finances as shown in the Town Reports of nearly 150 towns.[13] Of these towns, nearly fifty per cent had some indebtedness that was either illegal or improperly created. This, again, was not due to wrongful use of money, but to the lack of good accounting procedures, and the towns and the town auditors were in the dark as to where they were financially and how they could keep solvent. Much of this could have been corrected by the purchasing and keeping of proper account books.

Another study, made by persons interested in public accounting, recommended that the account books for town officers be of the binder-post type, with removable leaves. This would permit the addition of needed pages and the removal of old ones for storage in proper filing covers. The sheets should have enough columns so that each kind of expense item could be given its own column. For instance, the selectmen's books should show on each page, or double page, such items as salaries, office equipment, bonds issued, interest paid, bridge expense, roads, road equipment, etc., The expenditures in every column should be totaled weekly, and the total expenditures to date placed below it. Thus the selectmen could see at any time just where they stood in each type of expenditure. In other books, or on other pages, each of the items in a column could be broken down further, if that were thought necessary, with the weekly running totals kept up-to-date.

Accounts of this nature should be kept by officers handling money, and, in the ordinary town, would require but a few minutes a day, or an hour or so a week. The savings to the auditor in time and trouble at the end of the year would soon pay for the volumes, which are quite expensive, but which, with careful use, last for many years. A number of towns have purchased a full set of account books, and although some officers and townspeople may grumble at the prices paid, they will soon admit that there are fewer financial tangles than in the past. In case a town feels unable to buy all the books it needs, it would be wise to buy one or two books a year until the full set is available.

Accounts kept up-to-date greatly ease the task of the auditors.

---

13 *Governmental Costs and Taxes in 150 Vermont Towns*, Vermont Agricultural Experiment Station, Bulletin 546, September 1948.

There have been cases where the auditors have been forced to set up and fill out the account books for the year's business before they could see if the money had been spent properly; the accounts, or rather, lists of figures, were meaningless as they were presented for verification. Likewise, when in response to the biennial vote, the state auditor's men come to a town they can be of little help if there are no records of where the money went. Since the auditors have to certify that the accounts are in order, they have to take a real chance in instances where there is nothing for them to go on. Fortunately, conditions of this sort have become quite rare.

CHAPTER 12

Town Reports

In preceding pages references have been made to the Town Report, which is the official publication by which auditors fulfill their responsibility and report their verification of the town accounts to the townspeople. The Town Report is a pamphlet, sometimes large and sometimes small, printed annually before Town Meeting by the auditors in each town in Vermont. It is available for use at Town Meeting where it serves as a point of reference as the items of town business are discussed and voted upon.

Each report must show a "detailed statement of the financial condition of such town and such town school district for the fiscal year . . . a classified summary of receipts and expenditures, a list of all outstanding orders and payables more than thirty days past due, and show deficit, if any, . . . and such other information as the municipality shall direct. . . ."[1] Interpretations of this statutory requirement are almost as varied as the towns themselves, both in their method of summarizing receipts and expenditures and in presenting other information. The latter may include such items as a vignette of the history of the town, a map, graphs and charts, the town warning, or plans for the future. It is in the presentation of a clear financial statement and in the use of illustrative material to augment it that the auditors show imaginative understanding of their responsibility to the town and their capacity to do their work. The improvements discussed below are the product of the enlightened auditors of Vermont.

Thirty years ago nearly every Town Report in the state consisted only of long pages of dreary listings of the town orders, ar-

---

1 24 VSA § 1683.

ranged chronologically month by month. The provisions of the law were formerly interpreted to mean just that. There was no summary of the totals, and no relating of one department to another. The late James P. Taylor reported that most townspeople found their reports to be "as clear as mud." Any information derived from the reports was gleaned only after hours of intensive search. In an attempt to remedy this condition the Vermont State Chamber of Commerce, through its secretary, the same Jim Taylor, began a series of Town Report Contests in the early 1930's. These contests were based upon a series of ten points,[2] drawn up by Jim Taylor, and were intended, if followed out, to make the Town Reports more legible, more attractive, and more nearly an accurate picture of the town's doings. During the past three decades this work has borne fruit, and today, Vermont Town Reports are noted throughout the East for their contents and have won recognition in both national and regional contests. The movement for better reporting, thus begun to help Vermont towns, has been taken over by other states and in some instances these have left their teacher far behind.

---

2 The ten points were reprinted in 1950, by the Government Clearing House at the University of Vermont, and for several years were sent to all the auditors in the state.

JAMES P. TAYLOR'S TEN POINTS OF AWARD

1. Novelty and attractiveness of the cover.
2. Historical and statistical data about the town or city.
3. General appearance and orderly arrangement; including a table of contents listed by page number and an alphabetical index.
4. A balance sheet and a statement on financial status, for the past year.
5. Quality and substance in reports of the departments.
6. Schedule of the distribution of income and expenditures over a series of years.
7. Graphic display of financial and other facts through the use of bar charts, graphs, maps, etc., on indebtedness, delinquent taxes, relief, etc.
8. A striking summary of the most notable achievements of the past year.
9. Planning page devoted to a report of a local planning board, or to suggestions of an official or unofficial group concerned with the study of the needs and possibilities and future of the town.
10. A budget for the coming year.

As just mentioned, many towns have replaced the chronological listing of all the town orders with summarized statements of the expenditures of each department. In the best reports there is a brief statement of all the income and expenditures of the town, so arranged as to be printed on one page alone, or on two facing pages. This summary is most helpful when the page numbers of each of the supporting detailed departmental reports is given on each line of the summary. A few towns follow the summary with a clear and complete budget.

As mentioned above, the Town Report needs to contain only the summary figures for each account, leaving the detailed figures in the officers' books where they can be seen, if anyone feels the necessity of wading through them. What does count and is important is the total amount of money spent for each category of expenditure. Thus, it is better to know that three or five thousand dollars was spent for labor on a certain road, than to know the total number of checks or orders issued, which is almost the sole knowledge gained from the older listings. If the town wishes to know the total amount of money paid to each person who has received payment for work done, the matter could be handled easily. The name of each person who worked for the town could be set down, together with the total amount of money he had received during the year; this would be a short list since there are relatively few persons who work for the town for pay.

Several years ago the citizens of the town of Glover voted in Town Meeting to have the auditors include in the next year's report a chronological list of all the orders from January first to the last day of December. This the auditors did, although it spoiled their carefully prepared summary type report. They first put out their usual short, informative document and then followed it with the the lists of orders. The lists were prefaced by the statement, "Following the vote of the Town Meeting we have inserted these pages of orders at an extra cost to the town of $126." The town rescinded its vote at the meeting when the report was used and there has been no request for a return to chronological listing.[3]

If each department is given a place where a short report can

---

3 It should be pointed out that Glover is a small town, and that the sum involved was really noticed.

be made and a summarized account of its expenses and income shown, the inquiring citizen can find the answer to his questions. Tables of comparative costs for several years are helpful; they may either be with their department report or in a special section of their own. The tables may be pictorial presentations such as pie charts, linear graphs, or bar graphs which tell the story at a glance; the only requirement is that they be accurate and to scale. Some reports in the past have been misleading because the graphs were not prepared with sufficient care. The Bennington Report for 1941 remains one of the best examples for Vermont. The report contained 13 graphs which delineated Bennington finances from 1927 until 1941; the line which depicted the facts was red on a black chart and told the reader how the town's money had gone and in what amounts. No subsequent efforts have been so clear or so succinct.

In the state of New Hampshire in past years the reports have included an "inventory," i.e., a summary listing of the taxable goods of the town which gave the value of the various types of real estate, the number of cattle, other animals, etc., as well as other pertinent information, all in half a page. Such an inventory could well be added to Vermont reports and would improve their usefulness.

A detailed listing of the town assets is necessary, including town buildings and equipment, such as trucks. These should be depreciated properly year by year so that the list does not present a fictitious picture. The assets should *not* include delinquent taxes that are outlawed by the statute of limitations, while those that are included should be discounted to the extent that experience has shown necessary; if proper collections have been made there will be very little to count in in this field.

There should also be a story of the town indebtedness, if any. The total amount due, the interest payments to be made each year, the repayments of principal necessary, the proportion of the legal limit of indebtedness which has been reached, and the planned-for capital needs for the future should be shown in the Town Report. Since the law places a limit of ten times the grand list for bonded indebtedness,[4] the town should know where it stands in this respect. At this point it is well to remember that a comprehensive budget is a part of the document, but since it is discussed below, (See pp.

---

4   24   VSA   §   1759.

75-77) mere mention is made at this point. Also, somewhere in the document there should be a copy of the warning for Town Meeting, for to take a legal vote every item has to be listed in advance.

The value and attractiveness of town reports can be enhanced in many ways. As a public document the report should be prepared in such a manner that it will be picked up, read, used, and understood. First of all the reader's attention must be captured, and this is done most easily through an attractive cover. In comparing former and modern Town Reports the general attractiveness of the covers is the first change noted by the casual observer. Occasionally, Vermont towns have printed reports whose covers were really works of art, such as the silk-screen covers from Bristol. But a cover is not all that is needed. When the report is opened it must be readable and not a mass of smudged printing which repels the reader. The help of the printer should be sought to make use of his tricks of the trade — varying type sizes and colors, heavy type for emphasis, and use of interesting type fonts for over-all appearance. When the town auditors attempt to present a more pleasing report the town should give its enthusiastic support and not a cold rejection.

There should be a good table of contents and a usable index, so that any particular item can be found quickly. The latter greatly increases the usefulness of the report. At times an explanation of the cover is in order, particularly if it is a picture of a noted local person or of historical interest. A little of the town's history and some local statistics would be of value. These could include the population, the number of farms and industries, their valuation, the tax rate, and similar pertinent facts, preferably on a comparative basis over several years or decades. The Town Report gives an outsider the "feel" of the town.

One or more pages devoted to an account of constructive things accomplished in the town during the past year are in order, and following this, needs foreseen for the future. There should also be a map of the town in the report, showing its roads and points of interest. Maps for individual towns can be procured from the state highway department at little cost and plates can be made that will be usable for a good many years. Also, the office of the state auditor of accounts has issued a model town report, available from that office upon request, which has had wide circulation in the state. This model report stresses the financial aspects almost wholly, but were it followed closely there would be an excellent basis for citizen action in the Town Meeting. If the report is confused or obscure, the town does not have the knowledge of facts necessary for intelligent decisions.

CHAPTER 13

The Town Budget

In the preceding chapters the necessity for the proper and accurate accounting for the town's monies, together with the auditors' report of the same have been stressed. This, however, is only a part of the requirement. The town should have a budget, but few towns in Vermont have taken the steps to create a proper one.

A budget is a financial work sheet or plan upon which, once adopted, officers must base their operations. A good budget should include four sets of figures in item totals (1) the total actual expenditures of the year before last, (2) the figures proposed and accepted by the Town Meeting for the last year, (3) the actual expenditures for the past year, and (4) the expenditures proposed for the coming year. Also, the budget should contain the proposed tax rate based upon the prospective grand list. A tax rate must be accepted by vote of the town in order to raise the estimated revenue needed to cover the expenditures listed in the budget. If the tax rates for the past several years are included for reference it provides a valuable guide for the citizens.

Without these figures there is no true budget for the town finances. This fact is not understood widely, for in far too many Vermont towns the so-called budget is no more than a proposed tax rate on one or more such items as the general fund, town schools, or highways. Frequently, the town budget does not include the school tax. (A school district budget is required and is printed in another section of the Town Report.) This is bad, for unless all proposed tax rates and all proposed income and expenditures for the town are given in their grand totals, a false or misunderstood picture of town finances is conveyed to the citizens. It is here that the comparative figures for past years are so valuable.

It is true that different sets of officials are responsible for the several types of expenditures, but since their expenditure accounts are all a part of the town's finances, they should be collected and combined in one place. If this is done in the budget, with the supporting figures in the Town Report indicated clearly as to page, there will be fewer unanswered questions about the financial condition of the town. Also, with an accurate presentation of all the facts there is less likelihood of the town unwittingly voting itself into debt.

But, if the town is to have a budget, the question arises as to what person, or persons, has the responsibility for its formation. There is no set pattern followed in Vermont. In some towns the selectmen call upon the other town officers for the required figures, which are then compiled and presented in the budget. In other towns the selectmen and the town clerk study the town accounts and reach a set of figures; in still other places a general meeting of all the officers does this. A few towns elect a board of citizens who sit with selected officials to draw up the budget to present to the Town Meeting. A good variation of this procedure is found in Brandon, where a citizens' group has a great influence on the town's vote in all financial matters.

There is no best way to arrive at a plan which presents more than a proposed tax rate, or to assign responsibility for seeing that a good job is done. It is the failure to fix and assign responsibility which so often causes potentially good budget intentions to fall by the wayside. Often, an effective budget is achieved through trial and error; it is necessary to use plain common sense and to fit the budget form to the needs of the individual town. Even when, as in New Hampshire, a budget form is prescribed, townspeople seem to have as much difficulty with town finances as do Vermonters.

Whatever method is adopted for drawing it up, an effective budget does provide for fiscal planning. Planning through the budget makes it possible for the town to make provision for funds to pay off past debts, to pay current costs, and to provide for future needs — all in such a way that the ordinary citizen can understand the process. The only things which cannot be planned for are great natural catastrophes like the flood of 1927, or the hurricane of 1938, both of which washed out roads, bridges, and economic hopes without discrimination. But even here, planning and some flexibility can mitigate the disaster to the town.

A planned set of figures can help the town as follows:

First. The keeping of comparative records for budget purposes over a period of years will give the general trend of costs and from this the probable trend of costs in the future.

Second. The careful working out of expenditures soon will show which departments need more money and for what purposes. This will enable the Town Meeting to have a clearer picture of what the officers are doing, and this being true, policies can be discussed and votes taken on the basis of more information.

Third. A true budget will permit planning ahead of time so that no great or sudden increase in the tax rate should be needed, and perhaps even mean that fewer or no bonds will have to be sold. State law should be changed so that year by year a town can vote to lay by enough to provide the extra funds for normal improvement and expansion. Interest savings here could be an appreciable item. There is the major difficulty that whenever a town finds itself a little ahead in the way of funds, someone always moves to reduce the tax rate or to increase a questionable expenditure. It is this same type person who says that the work on a budget is unnecessary — an idea based upon a wrong conception of town finances.

Every town should insist that its officers prepare and present a complete budget each year. It is the budget which reflects fiscal security and safety for the town and keeps the citizens informed on financial trends as they appear. An adequate budget can be the means of saving a town from blindly creating unlawful indebtedness, and can protect individual town officers from the consequences of such an action.

CHAPTER 14

The Fiscal Year

In the discussion of accounting practices, budgets, and town reports, one matter was mentioned but not explained or discussed. This was the town fiscal year and its relationship to the business of the town. While the exact timing of the beginning and ending of the account-keeping for a town may seem of little importance to many persons, actually it is of real value in the proper functioning of town affairs.

In the past, all towns in Vermont had fiscal years beginning on February first and ending on January thirty-first. This timing just barely enabled the auditors to scrutinize the accounts of the town officers and publish the Town Report in time to give it to the voters before Town Meeting. When town business was simpler and the accounts were small, this time was not thought to be out of line, but as the complexity of activity and the increase in business began to close in, the auditors gradually found that there was insufficient time in the month allowed them to perform their tasks in the required manner.

Accordingly, the auditors began to agitate for a change in the fiscal year. This pressure was crystallized when the 1939 General Assembly provided that the town could vote to end its fiscal year on December thirty-first, or any other date in January, up to and including the thirty-first.[1] The town's decision was to stand until the town voted on a special article in the warning to rescind the action. Most towns have adopted the December date and the auditors have two full months to complete their work. The change was overdue since January thirty-first had nothing to commend it except that "grandpappy used that date."

Although a real improvement, the December date still leaves

---

1   24   VSA   §   1683.

much to be desired. First, the date has no real relation to the completion of town finances. Second, it makes it impossible for the town
to know where it is financially. Third, it is more costly than some
other time might be. In recent years there has been a change for the
better. The law was altered to require poll taxes to be paid by
December thirty-first if voters wish to vote in the March meeting,[2]
thereby making poll tax collection coincide with the fiscal year.

There could be no better illustration of the confusion in fiscal
years which still exists than is shown by the relationship between the
town and town school district. The town school district fiscal year
begins on July first, and the figures presented in the Town Report
are those for the fiscal year ending eight months before the Town
Meeting, i.e., the previous June thirtieth, plus the expenditures for
the six months ending December thirty-first — the end of the town
fiscal year. In addition, the expected expenditures for the remaining
six months of the fiscal year are tentatively set forth, but the tax rate
for schools, voted in the March meeting, is to take effect on July
first. Formerly, the vote was for the six months beginning with the
first of January prior to the Town Meeting, and for the rest of the
period then started. This proved so inefficient that the General
Assembly was induced to permit a town to vote an extra six months
of school money in any year, to be applied to paying the January
to June period of the current year and then voting the funds for the
town school year beginning July first.[3] This has been done in many
towns. This sequence leaves a large sum in the school account, and
some townspeople, not understanding the procedure, try to reduce
the school district tax rate because they have all these "surplus
funds" on hand. It takes considerable explaining by the school officials, and even then the confusion in fiscal years does not lead to
much satisfaction as far as the voters are concerned.

The confusion in town finances is also seen in the timing of
tax collections. The tax rates voted in Town Meeting for town expenses are retroactive to January first, but collections begin after
July first, sometimes in August or September. Even with installment
collections the taxes are not finally delinquent until the next January
first. State and federal taxes are payable at various times, with a July

---

2 No. 78 of the *Acts of 1957*, § 2, p. 53.
3 16 VSA § 3222.

to June fiscal year, and are not reflected in the town dates at all. Some of the cities in Vermont, the state government, and the federal government all use the fiscal year of July first to June thirtieth. Payments to the towns from both the state and national governments are made within these limits. Because of the methods of tax levying, collection, and of expenditures, December thirty-first is really little but a point in time. Would it not be well for the towns in Vermont in some given year to bring all their accounts to an end as of June thirtieth and then all proceed to the same fiscal year for all governmental activities?

This mention of the need for a different fiscal year is not made lightly. It is the result of the study of many Town Reports. It is almost impossible to make comparisons of the cost of government between any two towns, for their fiscal years and methods of bookkeeping vary. When compared in a given year two towns may seem entirely out of line because of the fact that January happened to be a month of heavy snows, and one town did not include it in its report because of its fiscal year. Unless citizens of a town can compare their finances accurately and regularly with their past reports and with other towns, no one can tell if progress is being made, or if the town is slipping into a financial morass.

Finally, this method of financing is expensive, because every year the town has to borrow money by short term notes "in anticipation of taxes." Tax money for the first seven or eight months of the year is nonexistent, since the collection period begins during the summer or early fall. This borrowing involves thousands of dollars per year, and in the course of time the loss in interest paid out reaches rather large figures. The collection of taxes in late summer and fall goes back to the days when Vermont was wholly rural and the only ready cash was derived from the sale of farm products after the harvests were in. This no longer holds true with agriculture producing only a fifth or sixth of the gross income in the state.

The time has come when serious thought should be given to a change in the date for Town Meeting; this date should be closely related to the total financial structure of the town and to the timing of the fiscal year. Without a change in the time of the March meeting the Town Report for the fiscal year, as proposed above, would be either for the period ending the preceding June, and wholly ancient history, or only be an educated guess for the coming year.

Neither alternative is an attractive one. The date of March meeting can be changed as the traditional date of convening the General Assembly was once changed; it would have to be authorized by the legislature and here a hoary tradition would be met head on. The rhythm of the seasons was the determining factor in the past, but changing conditions and all-weather roads have made a difference. If a different timing would make for better government and a more informed citizenry it would be worth the effort.

Specialized Officers

CHAPTER 15

Town Roads

I. THE ROAD COMMISSIONER AND THE SELECTMEN

Vermont early found it necessary to provide for the laying out of roads.[1] At first the selectmen had sole responsibility, but gradually it was found necessary to have other officers to carry out the work. On March 3, 1797, the General Assembly formalized this situation and provided for the appointment by the selectmen of "surveyors" who were charged with the care and maintenance of the town roads.[2] Today this office is known as that of the town road (or highway) commissioner. The statutes require that there be one or two commissioners for each town,[3] who are to be voted on at Town Meeting. A choice is permitted in that the town may either elect the one or two commissioners, or vote to have the selectmen appoint one or two. When the voting is done by a printed ballot and when there are villages in the town which do not pay the prescribed share of fifteen per cent of their road taxes for town road work, there must be a separate ballot for the road commissioner in the Town Meeting.[4]

In the past a good many towns chose two or more road commissioners, and a few still do so, dividing the town into districts over which each man has sole control. The only case in which this situation holds any logic is when the town is split into two parts by a difficult mountain range. When this is true the two separate parts

---

1 *Laws of 1779*, pp. 40, 41.
2 *The Laws of Vermont, 1808*, Vol. I, p. 408.
3 24 VSA §§ 711, 715.
4 24 VSA §§ 701, 719.

82

should be made into two towns, or the two sections should each be added to neighboring towns. The use of two road commissioners in an ordinary town is not good business; neither man can have enough to do, or be paid enough to make it worth his time to do the job, and the town suffers from lack of full time care.

The selectmen are responsible for seeing that the road commissioner does his job well.[5] If they have appointed him, they may remove him from office, if he is not doing satisfactory work.[6] Since it is the duty of the selectmen to lay out roads and to provide for hearings for damage to the property owner when new roads are opened,[7] the real work of the road commissioner is to act as the local technician for road work.

Since the office of road commissioner is an elective one in many towns, there can be few qualifications required for the candidate. This is probably a mistake, for with the coming of modern techniques of highway construction and maintenance, experts are required to do a good job. Too many towns in Vermont suffer from the lack of trained men and a too rapid turnover of commissioner; a few towns re-elect or re-appoint the same man year after year with beneficial results. If the commissioner is competent at all, the longer he serves the better he will become, within the limits of his physical ability. The state highway commissioner has said that continuing a town road commissioner in office generally results in the lowest cost highway work in the long pull.

Most towns spend a large portion of their town finances on their roads and this money should be well spent. All the money collected for this purpose must be set up in a special highway fund by the town treasurer[8] — the full amount must be turned over to this fund, since any deductions for payment ahead of time, for losses from delinquent taxes, or for collection charges must be borne by the general fund. The road commissioner has control over town tax money specifically voted for road expenditures,[9] and is to issue orders for payment for work done and for supplies used.[10] In his

5 24 VSA § 872.
6 24 VSA § 716.
7 19 VSA § 292.
8 24 VSA § 1574, and 32 VSA § 479.
9 19 VSA § 101.
10 19 VSA § 103.

work he is subject only to the general supervision of the select-men and to their approval of orders issued for his own salary or wages.[11] For his own protection every road commissioner should install an adequate set of books that can be kept easily. He should maintain his accounts in order at all times; his best answer to public criticism is a good set of books, with figures which clearly tell the story of the town road expenditures. To protect themselves and the town in the event that the road commissioner spends money wrong-ly, the selectmen are to require a suitable bond from him.

If, in spite of his record keeping, the road commissioner spends all his money and runs short of funds before the year is over, he is required to inform the selectmen of that fact and they have to main-tain the roads for the rest of the year, or to furnish the commis-sioner with enough additional money to do so himself.[13] If the selectmen have been so informed and fail to act, the road commis-sioner is not liable for any damage that may occur from an accident caused by the bad condition of the roads, nor, conversely, can the town then be liable for any costs entered into by the commissioner without the permission of the selectmen.[14] Whenever the selectmen are confronted with this extra expense, the funds must come from the general fund, as discussed above.[15] Any deficits due to this pro-cedure must be made up either by a specific vote by the town or by the selectmen adding five cents, or multiples of five cents, on the grand list to the tax rate already voted.[16]

It is the function of the selectmen to "lay out, alter, and dis-continue highways."[17] This duty is to be exercised either on the initiative of the selectmen when the "convenience of the inhabitants or the public good require it,"[18] or on the receipt of a petition from three or more freeholders in the town requesting that they take action.[19] When the selectmen receive a petition to lay out, alter or

---

11 19 VSA § 103.
12 21 VSA § 832.
13 19 VSA § 101.
14 *Ibid.*
15 24 VSA § 1526, See pages 33-36 above.
16 20 VSA § 1523, See page 13 above.
17 19 VSA § 292.
18 *Ibid.*
19 19 VSA § 341.

discontinue a highway, they first specify the time for holding a
hearing on the matter, giving at least twelve days notice to one or
more of the petitioners, and to those owners through whose land
the roads to be "laid out, altered or discontinued" run.[20] When, after the hearing, the selectmen decide that the public good or convenience requires action, they are to take the proper steps[21] and then
record their action with the town clerk within sixty days.[22] The
highways are to be at least three rods in width, with certain exceptions for trails and pent roads,[23] and they are to be surveyed at the
order of the selectmen or commissioners. The records of the survey and a statement of the place where markers and boundary
stones are erected must be filed in the town clerk's office [24] where
they must be recorded.[25]

If, as a result of the work, there are damages to be awarded
for loss of property or for inconvenience suffered, the selectmen are
to offer to pay a sum they deem reasonable before the highway is
opened.[26] At the same time that they lay out the road they are to
serve notice as to when the land is to be vacated and the buildings, if
there are any on the land, are to be moved. The period fixed must
be not less than two months for the land nor less than six months
for the buildings.[27] The selectmen themselves may move fences
and boundary structures, and if they do this, the landowner is to receive less money for damages than if it had been done in another
way.[28]

On the day a new highway is opened the selectmen must certify the fact and record it in the town clerk's office[29] and, in addition, within the space of six days, they must deliver a copy of the
recorded certificate to the owner or occupier of the lands which had

---

20 19 VSA § 342.
21 19 VSA § 343.
22 19 VSA § 344.
23 19 VSA § 294.
24 19 VSA § 296.
25 19 VSA § 297.
26 19 VSA § 345, and 24 VSA § 1621.
27 19 VSA § 346.
28 19 VSA § 348.
29 19 VSA § 349.

been taken for the newly opened highway.[30] If the owner is not satisfied with the payment proffered, he may appeal within sixty days after the highway opening to a justice court in another town[31] which is required to hold a hearing on the issue and to appoint commissioners to appraise the damages.[32] The commissioners are to give the selectmen and owners six days notice of the time when they are going to appraise, and after having made the appraisal they make their report to the authorities designated in their commission.[33] Ordinarily, this report is accepted and the matter thus settled. If this is not the case, the whole matter may be appealed to a superior court where the procedure is repeated.[34] If in either court the report of the commissioners is refused, the matter is sent back to new or the same commissioners for action "with instructions as justice requires."[35] When as a result of these proceedings, damages are finally awarded, the law says that if the petitioner prevails the town pays the costs, while, if the damages paid are smaller than offered, the costs are assessed against the petitioner.[36]

If, by any chance, the selectmen refuse to act on a petition, or within a period of three years do not build a highway that has been requested, three or more freeholders in the town may petition the county court for action.[37] The court serves notice of the petition upon the selectmen[38] and then proceeds to appoint commissioners to investigate and act in the matter, unless it can be shown that within five years two adverse reports on the same proposition have been made and accepted,[39] in which case the court acts as it pleases. If the commissioners are appointed, they act exactly as outlined earlier.[40] When there is a question of new roads needed in two or more adjacent towns, or of bridge construction on the town line, or of

---

30   19   VSA   §   350.
31   19   VSA   §   382.
32   19   VSA   §§   383 - 386.
33   19   VSA   §   387.
34   19   VSA   §§   421 - 424.
35   19   VSA   §   388.
36   19   VSA   §§   389 and 423.
37   19   VSA   §   461.
38   19   VSA   §   462.
39   19   VSA   §   463.
40   19   VSA   §§   464 - 471.

the change or discontinuance of a joint road, the statutes provide for similar actions on a joint basis.[41]

This brief mention of procedures available to the towns for their highways shows that every effort is made to prevent either the town or its citizens from being submitted to undue hardships. Always, it is true, the public welfare is put above that of the individual. The workings are often cumbersome, frequently archaic, and always slow, but they do provide essential justice for all parties concerned. Every stage of highway development is in the hands of more than one person and a majority of those persons resonsible has to disapprove or approve of the proposals. Of course, when there is no disagreement between the parties matters are settled in a hurry.

II TOWN ROADS AND HIGHWAYS

If a farm, or non-farm country dwelling is to have much value, it must be accessible both to the owner and to anyone else who wishes to do business with him. Accordingly, all town governments have found it necessary to build roads and to keep them open for the use of their citizens. In the early days of the settlement of the state, and even for long years thereafter, one of the common complaints heard was against the condition of the roads. Early travelers criticised the muddy tracks through the forests. During the long winters, in spite of the use of huge snow rollers on the roads, it was even more difficult to move about. Early Vermonters lived in virtual hibernation for the worst of the winter period, a way of life made possible by the long line of connected buildings, so often seen in New England, which made it unnecessary to go outside and into the cold.

The most recent biennial report of the State Highway Board[42] states that there are 13,629 miles of highway in the state. Of these, 2,073 miles are state highways completely controlled by the state; 2,533 miles are state-aid roads controlled by the towns but assisted by the state, which gives specific appropriations for that purpose; and 9,022 miles are town highways controlled and maintained by

---

41   19   VSA   §§   637 - 651, 681 - 682.
42   Biennial Report of the State Highway Board, 1961-62, p. 56.

the towns. Since 1946 there has been a change in road mileage figures, and transfer of the town roads to state control is quite marked and is the result of many factors. Although the total state mileage has decreased in this period by 540 miles, and the town roads have diminished by 635 miles, there were 270 more miles in state roads and 275 more miles in state-aid roads in 1962 than in 1946.

The figures that are important in this connection are those pertaining to town roads. Without these miles of highways many of the farms in Vermont could not market their produce and the farming citizens would be isolated, but even so these roads carry an insignificant proportion of the total traffic. In 1946, the State Highway Board reported the following statistics. At that time there were 1,803 miles of state highways and this was 12 per cent of the total highway mileage and carried 86 per cent of all traffic. There were 2,708 miles of state aid roads, comprising 19 per cent of the total mileage and carrying 11 per cent of all the traffic. Town roads, on the other hand, comprised 9,658 miles or 69 per cent of the state total, but these roads carried only 3 per cent of the traffic.[43] Later figures on the percentage of traffic carried by each type of road are not readily available, but the proportions have varied but slightly.

Because the terms "pent roads or trails" have been used and because they are unfamiliar to many persons, a brief description of their nature is in order. A public road or highway is land which has been taken by the government under the right of eminent domain, built up into a road, and is thereafter usable by any one who wishes to traverse it. The government, the town in this instance, is required to maintain this road, keep it in a safe and passable condition, and may be liable for damages when these conditions are not fulfilled.[44] No person may obstruct the highways[45] or obstruct travel upon them[46] without being subject to punishment. The key concept here is that the highways are maintained and are open to all, and may not have any obstructions upon them. A pent road, on the other hand, is a public way, but it usually is closed off with gates

---

43 *Biennial Report of the State Highway Board,* 1945-46, pp. 10-11.
44 19 VSA §§ 1371-1375, and 1391-1396.
45 19 VSA §   42.
46 19 VSA §   1501.

at either end and sometimes at intervening points.[47] The courts have upheld this interpretation. "All pent roads are public highways, though called in the early statutes 'private roads' — this is to say, they may be used by all — but they are not open highways."[48] "In the absence of official designation under this section of places where gates or bars may be erected on pent road, owner may erect them where they are reasonably necessary and do not interfere with reasonable use of road by others."[49] Also, "In absence of any prescribed regulations by proper authority, in respect to gates and bars across pent road, owner of the land through which the road is laid may erect gates and bars for the protection of his field and crops, if they do not interfere with reasonable use of road as a pent road."[50] The pent road must be maintained in a passable though not necessarily improved condition.

A trail, on the other hand, is a public right-of-way which requires no activity by the officials. Although the trail is used by passers-by at their own risk, they do have the right to use it. The trail may be fenced and barred like a pent road but the town has no responsibility for maintenance.[51] It gives access to property along its route, but if the landowners wish the right-of-way for their own use they must build their own bridges, or do any grading necessary. The town thus has no expense but does own the right-of-way.

(The statements in the paragraph above seem to have been the practice until 1963, when the Supreme Court of Vermont took a different point of view. *Whitcomb v. Springfield* (1963) 123 Vt. 395. The decision stated that "Not only do the abutting landowners resume domination over the land once used for the open highway, but not required for a trail, but upon application to the selectmen, the trail itself may be occupied and enclosed by them." The court also stated that a trail was a footpath and required an easement only over sufficient land to permit pedestrian travel. These two statements seem difficult to reconcile. Hence it will be necessary for

---

47 19 VSA §§ 1481-1483.
48 *Wolcott v. Whitcomb* (1867) 40 Vt. 40, at page 41, cited in Vol 6, VSA, p. 615.
49 *Judd v. Challoux* (1944) 114 Vt. 1.
50 *Wolcott v. Whitcomb* (1867) *Ibid.*
51 19 VSA § 293.

the General Assembly to clarify what has been existing law and practice by new legislation. The exact status of trails will thus not be known for some time since the current decision seems not to be in line with past practices and the general interpretation.)

Some three hundred miles of roads in Vermont towns are said to be actually in this condition of a trail without having been officially declared pent roads or trails by the selectmen.[52]. For this mileage the towns are receiving over $300 per mile as if these miles were actually used and fully maintained. The grants amount to over $90.000 and could probably be used for more productive purposes. In addition, at any time a family could move to a piece of property anywhere on these abandoned roads and demand that the roadway be put in shape to use. Even though they might pay not one cent of taxes, the town would have to bow to the demands. If these abandoned roads were officially declared to be trails, there would be no requirement to do any maintenance, and with a change of classification the town would be money ahead in the long run.

Town roads take about one-fourth of all the town revenues and thus the question of costs is always present. Since it is now necessary to have all-weather roads in the farm-to-market routes, and since new demands are arising constantly, there it little hope that either over-all or per-mile costs will decline in the future. Again referring to the State Highway Report of 1946, it stated that if improved gravel roads were to be extended to all the farms in Vermont, 2,641 miles of gravel would have to be added to the 3,759 already completed, and at an estimated cost of $7,925,000 at 1946 prices. It further stated that if the towns would use 60 per cent of their total sate aid money on this one project, they could complete the task in ten years,[53] but this monopolizing of funds for one use would starve all the other types of town road construction. The towns, of course, undertook no such costly program.

In 1952, the highway department estimated that to carry out a proposed 1949 program, "required to place 5,197 miles of town

---

52 *Burlington Free Press*, July 11, 1963, p. 1. The same source reported on September 23, 1963, that there were 781 miles of "untraveled highways" in Vermont. They were also called "Legal Dynamite."

53 *Biennial Report of the State Highway Board, 1945-46*, p. 13.

highways in a condition to adequately serve the traffic then using them," would cost $24,000,000,[54] a three and a half times increase in less than four years. Figures of such magnitude tend to frighten people and consequently are no longer cited. The nearly $400,000,-000 Interstate System in Vermont, for which the state is to pay approximately one-ninth, is merely added proof of the financial burden of highways.

The increasing costs of modern roads have long been more than the towns could carry. In order to prevent too great an increase in local tax burdens, the state has assumed a larger and larger proportion of town road support, first, by taking over more miles of roads directly, and secondly, by grants-in-aid to the individual towns. The aid program tends to equalize the burdens between the wealthier and poorer towns in the state, by taking money from towns whose people pay both increased local and state taxes, and paying it to the towns whose people pay lower local taxes (because of the state grants) and very little in the way of state taxes. Thus the increased burden for highways is not borne equally by the several towns. When the point of diminishing returns is reached in state aid and the costs of roads still increase, the state has to turn to the federal government for assistance. This means a matching formula and more national control, but it brings in more money.

This problem of control from the outside, whether it be Montpelier or Washington, is not taken lightly by Vermonters, because control of the purse is a powerful lever with which to force action. The townspeople are going to have to think this through very soon, as the introduction in the General Assembly of 1963 of the proposal to reduce the three-stage system of roads to a two-stage system of state and state-aid roads clearly shows. Continued town control of town roads won by a small margin. The retention of control of town roads, the determination of where they are to go, and the decision as to what type of upkeep to use will continue to be weighed against the benefits to be derived from more carefully planned projects, from centralized purchasing, and from better supervision.

There has been a long trend of regularly increased payments by the state to the individual towns for their highway program. This

---

54 *Biennial Report of the State Highway Board, 1951-52*, p. 33.

trend was finally broken when the General Assembly of 1963 froze payments to the towns for highways at the proportionate figures used for the purpose in 1962.[55] This was a concession to the supporters of the two-system highway proposals, and by stopping the granting of more and more payments to the towns may have been a turning point in Vermont highway history. Two cents of the current six and a half cents per gallon tax on gasoline is now designated for payment to the towns for town highway support,[56] and in 1962, these grants amounted to $2,742,821.76.[57] In addition, an emergency fund of $60,000 was set aside to help in hardship cases, and an additional ten per cent of the total two cent appropriation was set aside as a special bridge fund.

The apportionment to the towns is made on or before April 15, each year, and is reached on the basis of the road mileage of each town, as certified by a sworn statement to the State Highway Board by the selectmen on or before February 10.[58] However, the money is paid only when the town has spent at least $50 per mile of its own money for its roads, and is to be expended for construction or maintenance of the town highways on the recommendation of "a committee composed of the selectmen, road commissioners, and the district engineer."[59] Some of the apportionment, not to exceed an amount of $25 per mile,[60] may be used for plowing snow from the roads. If the cost of snow plowing becomes too great a hardship for the towns, up to one-fifth of the total apportionment may be used for that purpose. The special bridge fund is to be used to pay four-fifths of the cost of rebuilding bridges on town roads, when the span is more than four feet.

There is also an appropriation of two and a half cents of the gasoline tax for the 2,533 miles of state-aid roads. Yearly, the towns may receive up to $340 per mile for construction and maintenance of the state-aid roads within their boundaries, and in addition, up to $100 per mile for special work, signals, snow plowing,

---

55   No. 203 of the *Acts of 1963*
56   19   VSA   §   18.
57   *Biennial Report of the State Highway Board*, 1961-62, p. 56.
58   19   VSA   §   15.
59   19   VSA   §   18.
60   *Ibid.*

and the like.[61] In 1962, these two figures totalled $861,317.58.
This small figure is only that part of the appropriation spent directly
by the towns; the state administers the remainder. Bridges with a
span of not less than four feet are paid for from the state's share
of the appropriation up to the amount in excess of one dollar on the
grand list, which is the maximum charged to the town.[63] It is easy
to see why the towns feel these funds are important and why the
representatives of these towns in the General Assembly have insisted
on their right to determine the allocation of highway monies. Thus
the freezing action, mentioned above, is all the more remarkable.

The reverse side of the coin is that each town is required to
pay to the state a fixed assessment per mile of its roads. The assessment to any one town cannot exceed $300 per mile, $5,000, or $.20
on the dollar of the grand list.[64] The State Highway Board asks the
state treasurer to make the assessment against the towns, giving him
the official mileage of the town, as sent in by the selectmen. The
towns are assessed on or before September 1, each year, and the
town treasurer receives the notice, transmits it to the selectmen who
order the treasurer to pay the bill. If there are no funds available,
the selectmen must borrow the money and see that the treasurer
has placed the money in the state treasury before October 10th.[65]

In these transactions, both from the state to the town and from
the town to the state, there are seen interesting interrelationships between town officers, between town and state officers, and between
the towns and the state. Even though the law provides that none
of the payments to the towns be lump sum and automatic, made
only on properly authenticated vouchers, and sent in by the proper
officers, errors are made.

---

61 19 VSA § 17.
62 *Biennial Report of the State Highway Board,* 1961-62, p. 56.
63 19 VSA § 17.
64 19 VSA § 11.
65 19 VSA § 12.

CHAPTER 16

The Overseer of the Poor and Local Welfare

The office of Overseer of the Poor is an old one, because it has long been thought that local areas should take care of their indigents and other unfortunates. Bringing English precedents with them, the colonists in New England, from the very beginnings of their local government, made an effort to solve their welfare problems through the use of the customary and accepted officials. The office of overseer has remained a permanent fixture ever since.

In Vermont, the office is not sought, and a Town Meeting often has a great deal of trouble in filling the position. The town is required to elect an overseer each year, either a particular individual, or by a vote of the town, the selectmen or any of them, who must serve in this capacity.[1] When the town has a town manager this official is the overseer.[2] No matter who serves in the position, the work is subject to the general oversight of the selectmen.[3] The overseer must be bonded[4] and is one of the officials who come under the restrictions pertaining to incompatible offices.[5] He is seldom trained for his job since he is an ordinary citizen who has been drafted by his fellow-citizens for the office and who hopes to and is expected to get the work done as cheaply as possible. There is usually no salary connected with the task and the overseer has to donate his time; often he is an elderly retired person who has plenty of this commodity. When there is pay involved it is likely a sum too small

---

1 24 VSA § 711 (6).
2 24 VSA § 1236.
3 24 VSA § 873.
4 24 VSA § 832.
5 24 VSA § 737.

to mention in a voice above an embarrassed whisper. Only in the large cities and towns does the position become a full-time, paid office.

The law provides that the overseer shall have charge of all poor persons who apply for relief and shall support them as long as they remain the care of the town.[6] The overseer is to put poor persons to work if they are able and suitable work can be found, making a written contract with the employer,[7] binding them or their families out to work if necessary.[8] In older statutes the overseer was to prevent any such poor persons from "strolling" into other towns where they could become a charge upon that community.[9] To make certain that the town took care of its own and no others, the selectmen were empowered to "warn" anyone who came to town to leave on pain of legal action.[10] This was to prevent these "transients" from "going on the town." This antipathy toward the poor, and the old stigma that regarded helplessness or need as the result of a "sin" or as a punishment for something or other, resulted in very harsh treatment for unfortunates.

Although the listing of the duties of the overseer can be done very easily, it is much more difficult to explain their execution. A study of the Town Reports, and a summary of the discussion in the ordinary Town Meeting discloses that the prime requirement for the office is the ability to be "hard-boiled" with those who need help, to the end that the costs to the town be low. Several years ago the writer heard an overseer make the statement that five dollars a week was enough relief to keep a family with five children, and was a bit boastful of the fact that he had made such an arrangement with the somewhat feebleminded father. He had originally planned on giving him eight dollars a week, but had been able to "save" the town three dollars a week!

In normal times there are always persons in a town who need help because of illness, accidents, or events beyond their control. When there is a depression, as during the 1930's, or a similar catastrophe, the task of the overseer becomes most unpleasant and

---

6   33   VSA   §   704.
7   33   VSA   §§   961, 962.
8   33   VSA   §   963.
9   *Public Laws of Vermont 1933*, Sec. 3920.
10   *Laws of 1779*, p. 25.

difficult. During World War II the burdens of the office diminished because of the generally prosperous conditions and the consequent opportunities for gainful employment. However, it is not so much the ups and downs of periods of well-being or national disaster as the evolution in social patterns which is affecting relief programs, clear down to the local town and its overseer. Burgeoning aid and assistance programs financed largely by the state and federal government still leave gaps to be filled on the local level if humanitarian needs are to be met. Not all categories of need are provided for, there are delays while waiting to qualify for assistance, additional supplementary funds are required, and hospitalization costs are still a responsibility of the town. The overseer has the problem of transients, of temporary relief, and of the care of families of persons in trouble with the law.

The work of the overseer requires no small amount of paper work in recording the interactions between towns and the town and the state as they deal with recipients of relief. He must provide the state with proper vouchers and documents at legally stated times. The ordinary overseer does not have to, nor does he know how to keep careful case records on his charges. Some such records should be kept and would provide valuable knowledge when there is a change in overseers and when constructive, preventive measures toward rehabilitation are attempted. Ordinarily, the records kept show merely the number of persons aided and the costs involved. It used to be that all the names of persons helped and amounts given were printed in the Town Reports in such a manner and with such connotations that many families that could have benefitted from some help and thereby have pulled themselves out of their difficulties, took no assistance from the town because of pride and a refusal to be branded with the epithet "paupers." Often this resulted in further difficulties and eventual family disintegration. Today when federal funds are being used and payments made as a right of the needy individual, the former type of publicity is prohibited, and there can be rehabilitation where formerly there would have been only humiliation. Certain townspeople attack this prevention of publicity and a few towns still publish the list of recipients of local relief.

In mitigation of the position of some overseers it must be said that the other side of the coin involves the constant pestering of this official by persons who feel that the town owes them a living and who never seem to make the effort to help themselves. In many persons this is because of mental or physical deficiency, but in others it is sheer antipathy to work. Also the towns have their share of untrained, unskilled, and restless youth who exact their toll from their fellow citizens. Enough encounters with willing dependents upon the town, and their complementary personal abuse, and even the most humane and kind-hearted overseer begins to view the problem of welfare through jaundiced eyes.

There are two types of relief granted to those in need. They are known as "indoor" and "outdoor" relief. Indoor relief is that which is given in institutions in which the persons aided are required to live. Outdoor relief is that which is given to people in their own homes, or in any case, outside a formal institution. Today the larger portion of local assistance is of this type. In the past nearly all aid was indoor relief and was associated with the term workhouse or poorhouse.

Each of the towns was permitted to buy, build, or provide a town workhouse or house of correction for the reception and control of the poor. It was possible for several towns to join together to provide a cooperative workhouse.[11] During this era the "poorhouse" was considered the last word in disgrace, and for the aged, the poor, the diseased, the insane, and the crippled to be sent there was almost like receiving a death sentence. The indiscriminate collection of persons, without regard to age or health, could only result in horrible conditions. Public opinion slowly changed and forced an improvement, so that forty years or so ago the poorhouses, while not recommended as a choice place for residence were reasonably decent places in which to place persons who needed institutional care of the limited type which could be given there. The major difficulty was that the towns were too small an area to attempt to give this service and the costs were excessively high for results received.

While nearly every town once had such a town poorhouse, the pressure of changing times forced the closing of one home after another. The federal social security legislation sounded the final death knell and the towns gradually sold their properties, or sometimes turned the land into a town forest. One major exception to

11 *Laws of Vermont, 1797,* p. 281.

this trend was found in Franklin County where the Sheldon Poorhouse Association continued to carry on an acceptable program.
This was a joint project of several towns, and was the consequence
of the authorization found in the laws of Vermont from the earliest
days, and still permitted today.[12] Under the statutes each cooperating town can elect a superintendent of the poor annually, and
those so elected are then a corporation which operates the establishment and determines its policies. Each town is to contribute proportionately according to its grand list and may send its poor in
the same proportion. If some town fails to fill its quota, another
town may send an excess to fill the vacancies. It was this cooperation which enabled the Sheldon Association to care for the helpless
and needy of its member towns with greater humanity and less expense than found elsewhere. In the days when these local poorhouses were very prevalent it was unfortunate that more use was not
made of this authorization.

Today the Sheldon Home Association (as it is now called) is
having a hard time to keep going. New laws in Vermont and federal programs now provide funds and facilities which render the
same services in the form of outdoor relief programs. Because they
refer to specific categories of persons they are called categorical
relief programs, and they include Old Age Assistance, Aid to the
Blind, Aid to Crippled and Permanently Disabled, and Aid to Dependent Children. The first three are paid for by the state and federal governments, and the fourth requires the towns to pay one-
eighth of the costs only. Most of the recipients of this help remain in
their homes in their normal surroundings, and thus are happier
and better able to adjust to their lot. Under Old Age Assistance,
aged persons who have no relatives to care for them or who have
been unable to lay by enough to see them through the later years
are granted pensions and their self-respect is not lost. This same
factor enters into the program of Aid to Dependent Children; funds
are granted to those who care for the children so that the family
can be kept together in a home life that makes for fewer maladjust-
ments. Crippled children are aided, and the blind, so that they may
be self-sustaining, receive the same sums as the aged. There are still
gaps in the program, particularly with respect to the helplessly bed-

---

12   33   VSA   §§   1101-119.

fast and chronically invalided persons, but even here progress is being made.

Most towns now find their burdens for welfare and relief programs relatively light — ordinarly about eighty-five per cent of the costs are borne by state and federal funds. The town no longer needs to fear bankruptcy in caring for its poor and helpless.[13] This has removed a real burden from the overseeer who is usually able to report to Town Meeting that he has been able to fulfill the requirement of his office that costs be held low.

It is necessary to discuss a term which is constantly met with in legal suits and in any gathering of town officials. The term is "settlement" and means the legal residence of an individual and has a very great significance when it refers to the town's unfortunates. We have already seen how the laws of Vermont require the towns to be responsible for *their own* poor and needy. A person is required to live for three years in a town without receiving public assistance before he can establish a "settlement "there.[14]. This means that if, over a period of three years, a person receives any public funds for the relief of himself or members of his family from the town to which he has moved they are still residents of the town from which they came, and this former town is chargeable for their support. This situation is mitigated to some extent by certain laws enacted since the Social Security programs were devised to grant assistance as a matter of right, and not as charity to those in need. These laws specifically say that certain forms of these grants play no role either way in gaining or losing settlement.[15]

The settlement requirements often have unfortunate complications for the children of the poor. A family which is having economic difficulties moves away from its home in search of a job or better living conditions and, under such circumstances, it is quite probable that the family is short of funds. It sometimes happens that the overseer of the poor hears of their arrival in his town, and not wanting them to stay because he fears they may become a future

---

13   No. 273 of the *Acts of 1955*, pp. 273-274, provides for payment of hospitalization costs in excess of ten per cent of total town expenditures, excluding a few minor items.
14   33   VSA   §   701.
15   33   VSA   §   747.

burden on the town, offers them some help in getting on their feet. They gladly receive his proffered help because it is really needed, but in taking the "relief" they make it impossible to establish a "settlement" for themselves until after three full years have elapsed. Sometimes the helpful overseer will come around at intervals with help in order to keep them in a state of suspended residence. The overseer is taking a chance here for the law says that if he ". . . . wilfully furnishes relief with the intent and purpose of preventing a person from obtaining a settlement, [he] shall be fined not more than $100.00."[16] If the family moves on, the procedure may be repeated and the result is a family with no settled home for, if they have been away from their original home town for three years and have received no relief from it, they lose their settlement there.[17] Thus in the eyes of the law they become intra-state nomads.

In the past individuals or families who had lost their claim upon any one town for support were in serious difficulty. When after twenty years of wandering about the state, and even in other states where the same treatment had been accorded them, and the persons were finally in need of real help, it was the town from which they originally started that was legally responsible for their care. Often it was almost impossible to track this down. A family was sometimes picked up bodily and moved back to the last town of residence, the process being repeated until there was no place else to go. No town wanted or accepted the responsibility for their care. The effect of these rebuffs on family morale and on the children in the family can be imagined easily. Today the situation is different in that the family would be called "transients" and the state would pay for the costs of relief when the town or towns sent in the proper reports and vouchers.[18]

The three year settlement rule is still costly in terms of dreary human suffering and lost self-respect. As long ago as 1941, the report of the so-called Gates Commission proposed that "settlement" be required after one year in which no relief had been received. This, the commission argued, would remove much of the suffering that was then found. This proposal was opposed by the overseers

---

16   33   VSA   §   705.
17   33   VSA   §   701.
18   33   VSA   §§   821-827.

organization which favored leaving the law just as it was. In 1941, the Special Committee to Study Child and Family Legislation in opposing the proposal made the counter suggestion that the period for gaining "settlement" be reduced to two years, and that it take four years to lose settlement. In others words, a family that moved out of a town and did not return for four years would no longer be a charge on that town. If, in the meantime, the family had not gained a residence anywhere else, it would become a state charge as a transient family and the state would reimburse the town for the money it had paid out. Similar proposals have been made from time to time ever since but, except for permitting Old Age Assistance to be given to persons who had lived in Vermont for two of the three years preceding a request for the same,[19] no changes have been made. Settlement laws remain as they have been for many years.

Vermont is thus retaining laws that had their origins in the days when life was more static and it was difficult to move from place to place. Consequently the state has been forced to take over more and more of the relief burdens and further centralize governmental activities. The major difficulty in this centralization is that it tends to destroy a sense of local responsibility for the well-being of local townspeople; when the state pays relief costs there is a feeling that there is no need to worry about the matter. But the town is the place where the broken or needy home is and where its members have to live. Opportunities for decent living for all its inhabitants, and good schooling available to all its school-age children should be the concern of every community. Only by so providing, can a town hold its own.

---

19 No. 247 of the *Acts of 1957*, Sec. 1.

CHAPTER 17

The Constable

Another English office, that of constable, was brought to the colonies with the first immigrants. There were constables in the first towns in Massachusetts, and as the inhabitants spread throughout New England the office of constable migrated with them. The Constitution of Vermont mentions the office and gives the incumbent in each town certain duties in connection with the election of state senators and representatives.[1] Outside of this, there is no definition of his office or his other duties. An explanation for this must lie in the fact that when these statements were added to the Constitution in 1836, the duties were so well understood that it was considered unnecessary to say anything about them. This lack of definition is found in the statutes today where specific responsibilities are prescribed for the constable, and where references infer full knowledge of the office.

The constable is elected by the voters in each town at the Town Meeting,[2] and in towns with less than 4,000 inhabitants, if three persons so request, he must be chosen by written ballot.[3] One other constable may be elected if the town so desires.[4] When this occurs the first man chosen is called the first constable in the statutes, and is given added duties and responsibilities in consequence, all of which, however, may be assumed by the second constable in case of need. The constable is one of the officers required

---

1 Vermont *Constitution*, Chapter II, Sections 37 and 39, see also *Laws of 1779*, pp. 44-46.
2 24 VSA § 711.
3 24 VSA § 718.
4 24 VSA § 711.

to take the oath of office,[5] and before he may enter into his duties the selectmen must require him to give a bond for the proper performance of his duties,[6] or the office is vacant. This action of the selectmen is a requirement for entry into his duties[7] because the town itself is liable for any wrongful act committed by the constable.[8] The bond must be filed and recorded in the town clerk's office.[9] As with any other town office, the selectmen may fill a vacancy in the office, or even add special constables, by an appointment that is valid until the next town meeting, unless sooner revoked.[10] This appointment must also be filed with and recorded by the town clerk.[11]

The town may vote to pay a salary to the constable, or to permit him to retain as compensation the fees connected with the performance of the duties of his office.[12] When the town votes a fixed salary, the fees, as fixed by state law for each of the specific services, usually are put in the town general fund for the use of the town.

When a citizen has been elected to a town office and is not present at the meeting when the vote is taken so that he can accept or reject the office, it is the duty of the constable to carry the notification of the election to this person. Failure to carry out the duty promptly results in a fine.[13] Unless the town votes specifically for someone else to serve as tax collector, the constable automatically

5   24   VSA   §   831.
6   24   VSA   §§ 332-333.
7   VSA, Vol. 7, p. 386, citing *Weston v. Sprague* (1882), 54 Vt. 395.
8   24   VSA   §   834.
9   24   VSA   §   833.
10 24   VSA   §   1936.
11 24   VSA   §   1937.
12 24   VSA   §   932.
13 24   VSA   §   721. It might be worthwhile at this point to cite the section of the law relating to acceptance of office. 24 VSA § 722 *"Refusal to serve without excuse; penalty.* A person elected or appointed to a town or town school district office who refuses to serve or be sworn on demand of the town clerk or a selectman, without sufficient reason therefore, shall be fined not more than $10.00." This section was first enacted in 1787, showing that indifference to office or participation in local government is not wholly a recent phenomenon.

assumes that office, and is bound by all the laws and rules which govern the collection of taxes.[14] Many towns, however, fill both offices by electing the same persons to both positions. The constable shares with the county sheriff and his deputies the responsibility for collecting delinquent taxes by seizing and selling property by legal process when ordered to do so by the tax collector.[15]

The constable is required to post notices for the general election at least twelve and not more than twenty days before it is held, and before posting, this notice has to be recorded with the town clerk. For all towns with one polling place, the Secretary of State is to draw up the prescribed form to be posted and send it to each town. When there are two or more polling places the town clerk creates the notice.[16] It is the duty of the constable to preside at the general elections, and only in case of his absence or disqualification because he is a candidate for office do the selectmen or others take over the task.[17] For his presiding at the general election the statutes prescribe a payment of $6.00 per day, or more, if the town so votes.[18] The constable is held responsible for seeing that enough polling booths are provided in the town, that there are enough ballot boxes, and that no illegal ballots are deposited in the ballot boxes.[19] The constable usually watches the ballot boxes in the Town Meeting.

Although the constable has the miscellaneous clutch of duties described above, his chief duties today, as they have always been, are connected with law enforcement and the courts. As such an officer, his election must be certified by the town clerk to the county clerk as the representative of the state's legal process.[20] The constable is to bring lawbreakers before the proper authorities, and is to serve legal instruments at the order of the courts,[21] and to make returns on the action he has taken.[22]

---

14 24 VSA §   1529.
15 32 VSA §   5139.
16 17 VSA §§ 861-863.
17 17 VSA §   1002.
18 32 VSA §   1225.
19 17 VSA §§ 922-925, 17 VSA § 1931.
20 24 VSA §   1169.
21 12 VSA §   693.
22 12 VSA §   696.

The constable is the court officer for the justice of the peace court,[23] and may be appointed as the court officer of a municipal court.[24] He is required to take charge of the jury in a justice court and if he allows jurors to talk to outsiders he is to be fined for not doing his duty.[25] As court officer the constable serves legal papers and receives fees for the work. In this activity his jurisdiction extends throughout the state.[26] In some Town Meetings the townspeople vote to give the constable "the jurisdiction of the state," but this appears to be merely an affirmation of an already existing power. In cases of a "tumultuous or riotous assembly" of three or more persons the constable is to command them to disperse in the name of the state of Vermont, and if they do not heed his orders he may arrest any or all of the group and take them before a justice or magistrates court where they may be fined.[27]

The constable, along with the sheriff and certain other officers, is a truant officer ex-officio, and as such has all the powers to act as has the person officially appointed by the school-district directors to serve in this capacity, if he is a different person.[28] The constable may seize and bring before justices of the peace or a municipal court any gambling devices that he finds in use in a public place. The owners may be fined for such ownership and use.[29]

The constable and the other law enforcement officers are responsible for enforcing the laws prohibiting cruelty to animals.[30] In his law enforcement work the constable, like the sheriff, may call for the help and assistance of any citizens available, and if this request is refused the citizen may be fined.[31]

In all the functions of his office the constable acts for the preservation of the peace, somewhat in the broad manner in which the selectmen act in carrying out the general policies of the town. Both have extensive powers and exercise considerable discretion in ap-

---

23   4   VSA   §   507.
24   4   VSA   §   434.
25   13 VSA   §   301.
26   12 VSA   §§   691, 693.
27   13 VSA   §§   901-903.
28   16 VSA   §   414.
29   12 VSA   §   2137.
30   13 VSA   §§   407, 408.
31   24 VSA   §   301.

plying them. While it is true that in many towns there is little need for the constable in law enforcement work, it is comforting to know that there is such an official available in case of need.

CHAPTER 18

The Town Manager

Many times in the past when conditions became very bad indeed some guardian angel seemed to stand over Americans to show them the way out of their difficulties. This was the case with city government in the United States fifty years ago; after nearly a hundred years of corruption many cities had been brought to the verge of bankruptcy. Concerned persons were seeking a way out of the difficulty, and finally in their search they turned to a new system of government which was just then making its appearance in the United States and proving successful where tried. This was the council-manager form of government and is said by experts to be the only type of government to originate in the United States. All other practices and functions of government, including the use of a written constitution, have come to us from other peoples and other ages. The manager system is our own invention, and represents the American ideal of efficiency and economy of effort that has made this nation the envy of the rest of the world. The first city manager was hired in Staunton, Virginia, in 1907. Nearly 1900 cities, counties, villages, and towns in the United States had adopted the program and were using it in early 1963. The influence of these better governed units has helped to raise the tone of all governments in this country.

The theory of the council-manager form of organization is simple — government may be divided into two major fields, policy formation and the administration of that policy. Under the plan there is always an elected legislative body representing the public, and charged with the duty of formulating a program which it believes is best for that public. There is an administrator called the manager, chosen by the legislative body, who carries out the wishes of that body (the council). The manager may be removed by the council at any time for poor performance or for neglect of duty. By thus dividing the functions of government it becomes easier for the citizens to place responsibility. Failure on the part of either of the divisions is easily detected, and the public can demand remedial action. Because of this fact the story of manager-governed cities has, in most cases, been one of cheaper government in terms of money, and greater value received in terms of efficiency.

The Vermont General Assembly authorized the adoption of the town manager system by an act passed in 1917,[1] only ten years after the first manager had been hired in Staunton, Virginia. This was a good illustration of the fact that Vermonters knew a good thing when they saw it. The act, as amended, is now Chapter 37 of Title 24 of Vermont Statutes Annotated. Under its terms any town may adopt the manager plan of government by a majority vote of the people present at any regular or special meeting which has been properly warned on the subject of voting to adopt the town manager system. A special meeting to vote on the question must be called by the selectmen on the petitions of citizens of the town equal to four per cent of the votes cast in the last election for governor. The plan may be rejected in any properly warned meeting by a majority of those present and voting.

The law prescribes that the selectmen of the town which has voted to adopt the system shall "forthwith appoint a general town manager."[2] He may be any person who "shall be selected with special reference to his education, training, and experience to perform the duties of such office and without reference to his political belief."[3] The law also expressly states that he can be selected without any local residence requirements.[4] This is an important provision, for as a general rule it is best to have as a manager a person who has come into a community from outside its borders. The first town manager appointed is usually an outsider, but very often subsequent appointees are local men, chosen for political reasons and to placate local prejudices. When such an appointee is as good a person

---

1   No. 104 of the *Acts of 1917*.
2   24   VSA   §   1232.
3   24   VSA   §   1233.
4   24   VSA   §   1232.

as one who might be found outside the town, he is a jewel, and should be carefully treated, for other communities will be wanting to take him away at a much better pay figure. This pay question has been of real importance in Vermont, because some towns with a manager are so small that they can pay only enough to attract young or beginning managers, and soon lose them to larger places. This may have to be accepted and many towns reconcile themselves to the fact that their manager will have to make up in youth, vigor, and enthusiasm for lack of experience, which, once gained, will enable him to leave!

Every town, city, or village which has a manager still votes for the selectmen and other officers whose posts cannot be filled by the manager. In some cases the manager is elected to a specific position, such as town clerk or highway commissioner, as a replacement for one of these traditional town officials. However, each of the officers elected still performs his legal duties. But serving primarily in a position of general supervision, the manager carries out the mechanics of administration in the town and is of great help to the selectmen. If any officer interferes with him in his duties, after he has been instructed by the selectmen, it is the officer and not the manager who should be blamed if there are hitches. This interference explains some of the criticisms which have been directed at some managers, when in reality they should be directed toward those officers who did not permit them to do their work as instructed. Similarly, it will be found that in those towns where the manager has had a good record he has been permitted to act without interference; the selectmen have followed the wishes of the town as shown by the vote in Town Meeting and have set up a program of government, they have appointed a manager, told him what to do, and then have trusted him to do it. The manager has responded by satisfying the citizens who expected him to do the job.

Wherever a town manager is employed he is required to carry out duties which in the past had been divided among several other officers. The manager may not take over the duties of the school directors, but when asked to do so by them he may take charge of the repairs of the town school buildings.[5] The manager neither may serve on the board of civil authority nor fill vacancies in elective

---

5 24 VSA § 1234 (4).

offices.[6] While so stated in the law, common sense would forbid this since both tasks involve discretion and policy, and not administration.

The General Assembly has said that two or more towns may combine for the purpose of appointing the same town manager, and that when they do so, the manager is to perform the administrative functions of each of the combined towns.[7] This is a very wise provision, for many towns in Vermont are entirely too small to support a manager, even though they need this type of administrative help. By combining several small neighboring towns it is possible to have a large enough tax base to support good governmental services, and to afford to pay a salary large enough to attract a trained manager. Such a combination could bring greater efficiency at no more cost than is now paid for the several existing local governments. This authorization was not used until the spring of 1963, when the neighboring towns of Bethel and Randolph decided to appoint a joint manager. During the summer Brandon and Wallingford, towns thirty miles apart, decided to take the same step. These first experiments in Vermont need to be watched carefully because, if they succeed, many Vermont towns might profitably adopt this cooperative action as has been done already in Maine to the mutual satisfaction of all concerned. Cooperation might save towns that are slowly dying.

Before any town adopts the town manager system the townspeople should make a careful study of its tax base, its current and past budgets, and its probable future trends. If such a study points to too small a tax base it would then be time to approach a neighboring town and propose and ask for mutual action; it is an error to adopt a plan that cannot succeed because it is proportionately too expensive. In towns using the manager plan much of the criticism has been due to an original lack of understanding of the costs and the method of operation. There will be, ordinarily, no great reductions in costs but a greater effectiveness in the way the money is spent.

Where the manager plan has been in operation for some time the costs of government have been less than they might have been,

---

6   24   VSA   §   1236.
7   24   VSA   §§   1232, 1235, 1236.

since the continuous trend of small savings and improvements in techniques brought about by the manager has shown beneficial results. The town manager, who devotes full time to the task of running the administrative affairs of the town will do a more effective job than officers who are able to devote only a few hours a week, or month, to the task. He will be able to cut corners, and to have a long enough view ahead so that he can spend more at any given moment in order to save greater expenditures in the future. When this is understood, there will be less criticism on the part of those persons who expected immediate and dramatic reductions in costs. It is very seldom that a Vermont town has losses due to improper expenditures — rather, the difficulties stem from inefficient use of money.

In 1963, there were managers in 39 towns or villages, or both, in Vermont. There are a few places which have abandoned the plan after adopting it, and a few which have returned to the system after abandoning it for a time. Every year there is considerable discussion in one or more towns about the value of the manager system, and the principle of "contagious diffusion" seems to guarantee a continued interest and a regular expansion in the system. The record of good government, in most of the towns that have made use of the enabling act[8] and hired a town manager, is impressive.

A. OFFICERS' SALARIES

When the first *Constitution of Vermont* was drawn up in 1777, the drafters were engaged in a struggle to insure their independence. They were free men who had a sense of grievance against the established government of England. It is not surprising that they carried some of this feeling over into their thinking about their own new government, expressing it in the statement that "that government is best which governs least." To make certain that this concept would not be forgotten the convention placed in Section XXXIV of Chapter II, of the first *Constitution,* the following sig-

---

8   24 VSA   §§   1231-1243.

nificant clause: ". . . and whenever an office, through increase of fees or otherwise, becomes so profitable as to occasion many to apply for it, the profits ought to be lessened by the legislative."[1] Then, and now, it was also stated that every man should have an occupation of his own, and that this should be the real source of his income. When any man did go to work for the government, at the expense of his own affairs, it was stipulated that he should have a fair recompense for his pains.[2]

Unfortunately, the simple governmental practices of the 18th century no longer suffice for an industrialized economy and most government officers can no longer do their work in their spare time and in "after hours" leisure periods. People demand services and protections that were unheard of in their grandfather's day, and carrying out these demands becomes a full-time job. Even though there has been this increase in demands, there has been a delay in realization that it does take full time to administer these government services. This lack of perception is seen in the fact that many offices are still considered part-time jobs, and yet when the underpaid or non-paid officials act in conformity with this principle, the community becomes incensed at the lack of official action. There is a reflection of this in the many towns where no sustained effort has been made to pay for the injury to an official's private interests when he works for the town, let alone payment of a stipend for time actually put in.

In this situation lies one of the reasons for the hesitation of many young people to assume the duties of a town officer. A conscientious carrying out of the town's affairs means the reciprocal slighting of the officer's own business. When there is a choice between feeding one's own children or going all out for a town, the former usually wins. It is thus very important to consider the necessity of paying adequate sums to town officials to make the job a worthwhile one. Some towns have tried to alleviate the weakness of low pay by electing one person to several compatible offices, and paying enough for the several posts to provide a small and comparatively adequate income; here an effort has been made to provide

---

1 This clause is now a part of Section 57 of Chapter II, of the present *Constitution of Vermont.*

2 *Ibid.*

for better administration by enabling a person to spend full time in the public service. But if the person in question is untrained he may be unable to handle a series of different tasks.

A study of Vermont town reports in any given year reveals that salaries paid to town officers are entirely too low. It is true that many towns now pay all they think they can afford, but the figures are still inadequate. Such towns would do themselves a good turn by joining with other towns in hiring a joint town manager. Together they could pay an adequate salary and probably still pay less than they are now paying when they give all their officers a mere pittance. They would also get full time services instead of part-time.

No set figures can be given for the salaries which ought to be paid in any town for the amounts will depend upon work to be done and the financial position of the community. The decisions should be based upon the average fair wage in the town, the local cost of living, and similar factors. Thus an income for an officer in a small town amounting to half of that of an officer in a large town or city might be fair, and still give a comparable standard of living. Each case has to be handled on its merits, and each town ought to do the best it can so that town officers can make a respectable living. They should have no other contact with the overseer of the poor except that of being a fellow officer.

CHAPTER 19

Minor Town Officers

The discussion so far has been concerned, for the most part, with the duties of the major elected officers of the towns — those officials whose activities are most likely to affect the lives of the citizens. Attention must now be given to some of the many minor officers, and to the special roles which they play in self-government. Every town in Vermont has a certain number of appointed officials in addition to those voted upon at Town Meeting.

Throughout New England the number of minor officials has grown and ebbed with the changing times. Some of these positions date back to colonial days; others are of recent origin; and still other posts have been abolished as no longer being of value. In Vermont all these offices have been authorized, at one time or another, by the General Assembly and this authorization has given them validity. In this respect Vermont differs from New Hampshire, which by an "omnibus clause" permits towns to create offices for which a need is felt. Not the least intriguing of these special posts across the Connecticut river was the one which was called "picker of brown tailed moths."

Perusal of older statutes shows an officer for the control and regulation of almost every type of activity. Those who complain that today's government interfers unduly with the citizen's private affairs are not very much aware of the background of our state. The writer likes the sound of the titles of some of these old offices— the Sealer of Leather, and the Culler of Hoop Poles, Staves, and Headings. The latter was an important person when nearly all shipments were in barrels; hoops, staves, and headings were the component parts of that useful article. The office of Hearse Warden was created to prevent the local undertaker from having a mono-

114

poly at a time of sorrow. The list of these minor posts is long and interesting, even if largely antiquarian, and some of the existing remnants will now be discussed.

A. FENCE VIEWER

One of the oldest, as well as one of the most important of the appointive offices is that of Fence Viewer, an office that goes back to the first days of the New England colonies. While city humorists and uninformed persons consider this post the subject of much mirth and attempted wit, the officials and citizens who are in need of a fence viewer know the importance of the position. In Vermont, following the election of the new member at Town Meeting,[1] the board of selectmen, as soon as it has met and organized, appoints three fence viewers. The importance of this office is shown by its being one of the listed offices for which an oath is required from the officer-elect before he enters into his duties.[2]

An old saying often quoted in terms of approbation by Vermonters states that, "Good fences make good neighbors," and the presence of neat fences and hedgerows attests to its acceptance. There are times when fences get into disrepair, or a landowner refuses to build a line fence, and then trouble arises between the adjoining property owners. The long long list of court decisions on this question and the extensive sections of the law on the duties of the fence viewers[3] show the seriousness with which this matter of fences is taken. It is to prevent the necessity for legal action that the fence viewer comes into the picture — but often too late to settle the dispute amicably. Although in any given town the fence viewers may not be called upon for their services over a long period of years, nearly every year some of these officials in some towns are asked to decide questions about fences, and their decisions when filed and recorded in the town clerk's office become binding legal actions. The one thing the fence viewers cannot do is to establish boundary lines for property; that is the duty of other officials,[4] and

---

1 24 VSA § 871.
2 24 VSA § 831.
3 24 VSA §§ 3801-3817.
4 27 VSA § 4.

is set forth in another section of the law.[5]

A variation of the above is seen when the property line lies over water, or when for some other reason it cannot be followed. In these circumstances the fence viewers are to determine where the fence is to be built and how much each adjacent landowner is to pay for its upkeep. The line is to be made as close to the real line as possible and the fence viewers are to fix the area of the land that, although belonging to one landowner, is behind the fence and is used by another owner. They are also to provide for whatever settlement of claims arise out of this fact in the future.[6] The decisions made are to be final and binding.[7]

Legally, fences in Vermont are to be at least four and a half feet high and of such construction that sheep cannot escape.[8] The requirement for height goes back to October 1780, when the General Assembly decreed "that no fence or fences within this State, shall be deemed lawful, unless it be four feet and an half high, well built with logs, rails, stones, or boards, or other fence equivalent."[9] The land owner is not required to build a fence along the road, but must do so between his and his neighbor's property.[10] This provision goes back to the older English practices. When there is no fence along the highway any person driving animals along the road has only to be reasonably careful that the animals do not stray on the property. If there is a fence "they enter at his peril."[11]

Each property owner is required to maintain equal portions of the fence along his land boundaries, or pay his fair share of the costs if the work is done by others. If either owner fails to cooperate in this mutual sharing of the burdens, and troubles appear as a consequence, the fence viewers are called in. After due notice to both parties that they are about to take action, the fence viewers proceed

---

5 See Vol. 7, VSA, p. 585 where these citations show the problem. *Campbell v. Campbell* (1887) 59 Vt. 667, and *Shaw v. Gilfillan* (1850) 22 Vt. 565.

6 24 VSA § 3806.

7 24 VSA § 3805.

8 24 VSA § 3801.

9 *Vermont State Papers*, William Slade, Jr., Middlebury, 1823, p. 405. Hereafter this publication will be cited merely as *Slade*.

10 24 VSA § 3802.

11 24 VSA § 3801.

to examine the fence and then give to each person his fair portion of the fence to maintain, or they fix the proportionate value of the repairs. The record of this action is placed in the town clerk's office and is binding then and in the future.[12] If, instead of fighting it out, each party signs an agreement about the fence and the document is then recorded with the town clerk the arrangement is to be held valid in all cases of argument in the future.[13]

If there is a pasture or other land that has no boundary fence, neither owner may turn stock out to graze unless both have agreed to use the land without a fence. If they cannot reach an agreement, the fence viewers, after notice to the party who has not appealed, are to fix the number of animals that each may put into the pasture. This decision in the matter is to be recorded with the town clerk and is to be final.[14] If the property or stock of a landowner or tenant is injured because of the failure of a property owner to keep his fence in shape, the delinquent owner may be sued for the damage suffered.[15] Many court decisions have made this principle very clear. At the same time, the law is specific in the terms which prohibit the erection of "spite fences" which can interfere with the view, the light, or the air to which a person is entitled.[16]

As times have changed the work of the fence viewer has declined in importance, and few people know about the office and its duties. When fences were made of rock or wooden rails, it was very difficult to keep livestock in the pasture, and to prevent damage when it broke out. With modern fencing this problem has tended to decline. A writer discussing fence viewers in New Hampshire upheld this idea when he said, "It would be interesting to compare the decline of this office with the growing abundance of modern fencing material." But as long as there are individual property owners there will be disputes over the costs of keeping fence lines in order and someone will have to settle them. Until there are changes in the statutes the fence viewer will be called on at irregular intervals to do what neighbors have forgotten to do, or refuse to do.

------

12   24   VSA   §   3811.
13   24   VSA   §   3812.
14   24   VSA   §   3804.
15   24   VSA   §§   3807, 3808.
16   24   VSA   §   3817.

B. TOWN AGENT

In Vermont since 1779,[17] there has been statutory provision for an officer similar to the town agent. From colonial days on, this post has been in existence throughout New England, but under various names. The exact position as it is found in Vermont today dates from the period 1824 to 1840, and it appears first in the *Revised Statutes of Vermont* of the latter year, but not in the former. Somewhere in between the two dates a change in classification was made which the writer has not yet discovered. Then, as now, the Town Meeting was to elect "a town agent to prosecute and defend suits in which the town or town school district is interested."[18]. The courts of the state have held that this requirement has to do with civil suits and not with criminal cases.[19] Criminal cases are the responsibility of the town grand juror, mentioned below.[20]

It is the responsibility of the town agent to prosecute and defend cases only, and not to give advice ahead of time, even if it might prevent suits. The town agent may begin a suit and is responsible for its completion, and may, in certain cases, turn the case over for arbitration. He does not have to be a lawyer but is authorized to hire counsel who will be able to argue the case. This is the usual practice in Vermont for rarely is the man who is elected to the post trained in the law. It is an advantage for town agents to be able to hire one of the few but widely used attorneys who have specialized in municipal law. To master the intricacies of legal procedures in local government requires more time and effort for specialization than most lawyers can devote to the task.

If the agent is negligent or if he refuses to take action when necessary the selectmen of the town have the right to hire counsel for the case. This is in full conformity with the selectmen's obligation to see that all the business of the town is transacted properly, and clearly illustrates another ramification throughout local government of the selectmen's office. The selectmen may not themselves

---

17 See *Laws of 1779*, p. 6, and *Laws of the State of Vermont, 1797*, p. 300.
18 24 VSA § 711 (12).
19 See *Burton v. Norwich* (1861), 34 Vt. 345, 351.
20 See the annotations to 24 VSA § 711, at page 372 in Vol. 7.

be town agents, as the offices are legally incompatible,[21] but they may be asked by the agent to hire counsel for a town case. A failure of the town agent to protest the action of the selectmen when they act on their own motion is presumed to be consent through silence, and the agent may not later claim he was overruled.[22].

Few town agents are overworked these days in carrying out the duties of their office. Nearly all the Town Reports show that the town agent's report for the year, when it appears, consists of the statement that there has been nothing for him to do. On the other hand, in some rare instances cases arise which keep the agent busy for several years and involve the expenditure of considerable sums of money. In these instances the annual report may be watched for with considerable pecuniary interest. In the cities of the state the duties of a town agent are assumed by the city attorney and he has full charge of the legal work of a civil nature for the city.

This short recital of the present-day duties of the town agent is a far cry from the days when agents were elected by the people to go to England to plead the causes of provinces or areas of the provinces. The work of these men was often to no avail, and their supporters were left with the task of settling their accounts. On the other hand, there is no doubt that the experiences of these men, when shared with their fellows, acquainted them with the old country and the outside world.

C. TOWN GRAND JUROR

While few persons know about the work of a town agent, nearly everyone knows about the prosecuting attorney, in one or more of his varied titles. These officials who handle the criminal work on the local level in Vermont are known as town, or city, grand jurors, and on the county level as state's attorneys. One or more grand jurors are elected each year by the Town Meeting.[23] When there are minor crimes in the town the grand juror makes the presentment or charge and gives it to a justice of the peace or to a municipal court,

---

21 24 VSA § 737.
22 *Burton v. Norwich* (1861), 34 Vt. 345, 348.
23 24 VSA § 711 (11).

and then may follow it up till settled.[24]   There is thus a clear-cut distinction in the two offices. The town agent is to prosecute and defend civil cases involving the town; the grand juror is to prosecute cases against persons charged with a breach of the peace.[25] The latter officer has the most work to do, although as a usual thing neither will be called upon often enough to learn his job well.

D. TRUSTEE OF PUBLIC FUNDS

A minor office which has a varying significance in the towns of Vermont is that of trustee of public funds. If the town has decided to relieve the selectmen of the duty of handling trust funds the Town Meeting may elect a trustee of public funds each year.[26] There is a board of three members, with a three year term for each, one member retiring each year.[27] This board has charge of all town property and funds from which income may be realized, including cemetery trust funds, unless the granter has specified differently.[28] The board is charged with investing the funds and otherwise prudently handling the sums entrusted to it. The types of investment are prescribed by law,[29] and the trustees must be bonded.[30] If the town has kept its accounts in order it may have an accumulation of considerable sums that have been given to it through the years, so that it is well for the town to consider with some care the choice of its trustees of public funds. The board, or the selectmen, must report to the Town Meeting each year on their handling of the trust.[31]

In 1957, the General Assembly changed the law pertaining to investments. This was due largely to the need to legalize the work of one trustee in the state who had not followed the law. A retired investment broker, he had very prudently exercised his accumulated

---

24 13 VSA §§ 5504, 5505.
25 13 VSA §   5508.
26 24 VSA §   711 (13).
27 24 VSA §   2431.
28 *Ibid.*
29 24 VSA §   2432.
30 24 VSA §   2433.
31 24 VSA §   2434.

wisdom and enhanced the value of the town's holdings. The increment had been considerable but, because it did not follow the statutes, most of it had been illegal. When the trustee became cognizant of the law he protested its terms, and argued so cogently before the legislative committees and the interested state officials that the law was changed and he was thus made an honest man again — to the resulting benefit of his town and all the other towns in the state.

E. TRUSTEE OF PUBLIC MONEY

An interesting sidelight on public funds concerns the United States Deposit money. In 1836, the national government was confronted with an unprecedented surplus of funds that it did not know how to use. National officials finally decided to pass out this extra money to the states. In due course Vermont received its share and has held the money ever since. It constitutes a portion of the permanent school funds of the state. Any town was privileged to borrow some of this money in the proportion which its population bore to the total population of the state, and to pay interest to the state for it. In recent decades the interest was five per cent. To handle funds received in this manner the town was required to elect a trustee of public money.[32] In 1938, there were 57 towns in this category, 12 in 1946, and the 1962, *Report of the Treasurer and Commissioner of Administration* showed that in 1961, the last town, Newark, paid back what it had borrowed so long ago.[33] The repayment was good business for the towns, since for a long time they had been able to borrow money at less than five per cent. Thus it is that a program lasting for 125 years has come to an end, and with it another of the minor town posts.

F. CEMETERY COMMISSIONERS

Every town may choose a board of cemetery commissioners, [34]

---

32 24 VSA § 711 (14).

33 *Report of the Treasurer and Commissioner of Administration, 1962*, p. 134.

34 18 VSA §§ 5373, 5367.

if it does not wish to assign their functions to the selectmen.[35] There are five commissioners, with a five year term of office, one retiring each year [36] except in the case where the town decides that three members are enough, and then the terms are reduced correspondingly.[37] The new member is chosen by the Town Meeting.[38] This board is placed in charge of the public burying grounds of the town, is responsible for their proper upkeep, lays out new areas when the need arises, and purchases and sells land.[39] The board does not control the money used for these purposes since it is already in the hands of the trustees of public funds, or, in a few instances, the treasurer.[40] The cemetery commissioners must report to the town each year, detailing their activities, and setting forth proposals for the future.[41]

G. HEALTH OFFICER

The local health officer is an appointed official with important functions. Since the passage of No. 113 of the *Acts of 1902,* he has been appointed by the State Board of Health upon the recommendation of the selectmen of a town.[42] If the selectmen fail to act, the state board of health may act on its own motion, after thirty days notice to the selectmen.[43] Since 1961, several towns and cities may combine to form a health district with added duties and officials—a real step forward.[44]

The local health officer and the selectmen of a town, or the councilmen of a city, constitute the local board of health,[45] and have rather extensive powers. The health officer may make sanitary in-

---

35 18 VSA §   5381.
36 18 VSA §   5374.
37 *Ibid.*
38 24 VSA §   711 (15).
39 18 VSA §   5384.
40 18 VSA §   5348.
41 18 VSA §   5379.
42 18 VSA §   601.
43 *Ibid.*
44 *Ibid.,* (b).
45 18 VSA §   604.

spections of any place or material which he suspects may be detrimental to the public health.[46] He can order the destruction or removal of nuisances, [47] but only after the approval of the selectmen, if an expenditure is involved.[48] He can forbid the holding of meetings and assemblies if the state board of health informs him that the action is necessary.[49] He may quarantine persons and homes for infectious diseases,[50] and can order proper sewer connections made.[51] All in all, his duties are very important for the welfare of the community.

Unfortunately, most of the town health officers in Vermont are not doctors; there simply are not enough doctors to supply the needs of the towns. One can sympathize with the layman who is charged with the technical duties of the health officer without having had the training which would qualify him for the post. Somewhere and somehow rural Vermont must secure more trained medical practitioners if local health problems are to be handled properly. In line with the provision for health districts, the authorized union of towns[52] may be a step in this direction since it takes an adequate tax base to support trained officials.

H. TREE WARDEN

Mention of the tree warden, a minor town official, frequently causes merriment among the uninformed. This officer is appointed by the selectmen and holds office until his successor is appointed and qualified.[53] The post seems to have been created by No. 76 of the *Acts of 1906,* and was designed as a means of protecting the trees that border the public highways of the state. All public shade trees (those growing on public property along roads and highways) except those in public parks and subject to the control of park com-

---

46 18 VSA § 606.
47 18 VSA § 610.
48 18 VSA § 615.
49 18 VSA § 607.
50 18 VSA § 612.
51 18 VSA § 618.
52 See p. 7 above
53 24 VSA § 871.

missioners, are under the care of the tree warden.[54] He is responsible for the expenditure of money appropriated by the town for the
planting and maintenance of public shade trees,[55] and for extermi-
nating insect pests threatening these trees.[56]

A town may vote to raise funds at a rate not exceeding one
cent on the grand list to pay premiums to or otherwise induce persons to plant shade trees on public lands adjoining their property.[57]
The town may also vote to appropriate a sum of money of not more
than fifty cents for each ratable poll, which the tree warden may
use to plant shade trees on public ways, or with the consent of the
property owner, on private land within twenty feet of the public
way.[58] As a rule public shade trees may not be cut or marred without the written permission of the tree warden, [59] while public shade
trees in a residential area are not to be removed or cut down without a public hearing on the action.[60] The trees may be trimmed
without a hearing, (occasionally the "trimming" leaves little behind
but a mutilated stump,) but no other action is authorized. Money
may be appropriated for the extermination of insect pests, and the
tree warden can cut or remove any infected trees, or those which
may become so, unless the abutting property owner satisfies the
warden that he has successfully controlled or exterminated the
pests.[61]

I. TOWN FIREWARDEN

While the duty of the tree warden is to help preserve the beauty
of the town, another officer is charged with helping to preserve its
forests. This official is the town firewarden whose home, with its
identifying sign placed along the road, is so often seen on drives
about the state. He is appointed by the state forester with the ap-

---

54 24 VSA § 2502.
55 24 VSA § 2503.
56 24 VSA § 2511.
57 24 VSA § 2503.
58 24 VSA § 2507.
59 24 VSA § 2508.
60 24 VSA § 2509.
61 24 VSA § 2504.

proval of the selectmen and serves until a replacement is appointed and approved.[62] If fire conditions warrant it, the state forester may appoint two or more deputy firewardens who have equal authority and responsiblity with the regular firewarden.[63] The town is to pay the warden, and any helpers he has called out, according to the town's regularly used hourly pay scale. In any given year the cost of these payments shall not exceed ten per cent of the grand list.[64] Additional costs are to be paid by the state, agreeable to stipulated circumstances.[65]

The firewarden issues permits for burning waste in the forest lands; he is required to report all fires in woodlands in the town; and he has full police power to call for help in putting out forest and brush fires, and to take steps necessary to control further spreading of the fire. The need for, and the value of firewardens has been demonstrated during every period of prolonged drought in the state. Their powers to control burnings, together with the governor's power to close the woods to entry and to prohibit fires in forest areas,[67] are about all the protection that can be given to the woodlands of the state without the full cooperation of the public in refraining from committing acts which may result in timber fires. To bolster the orders of the governor and the firewardens, there is a fine of up to $50 and a short prison sentence for leaving a fire burning in the woodlands of the state.[68]

J.   POUND KEEPER

Few officers can cite a longer tradition of office, and few are now of such an innocuous nature as the pound keeper. When wealth was often measured in animals, and life itself depended upon a supply of food on the hoof, it was important that there be regulations concerning the treatment accorded to lost or strayed animals.

---

62 10 VSA § 1481.
63 10 VSA § 1493.
64 10 VSA § 1485.
65 10 VSA § 1487.
66 10 VSA § 1483.
67 10 VSA § 1502.
68 10 VSA § 1499.

Thus it is that for centuries there have been detailed regulations in these matters. In Vermont, these rules, together with those calling for the building and maintenance of good fences to prevent animals from straying, have from the very beginning of the state furnished a sizeable portion of the laws.[69] Because livestock was unable to read the rules and seemed to have an antipathy against staying inside their master's fences, the office of pound keeper was essential.

The town's pound keeper is appointed by the selectmen.[70] Every town in Vermont is required to have and to maintain at least one, and if necessary, two or three "good and sufficient pounds" for taking care of roving livestock, and if they neglect to have such a pound for a six months period at one time "it shall be fined $30.00.[72] If there is no town pound, then anyone who picks up an estray on his land may impound the animals in his own barn or field.[73] He must carry out the terms of the law if he does so.

A person who picks up and impounds an animal must (the law and judicial decisions are unanimous on this point) feed and care for the creature according to the time of the year and the customs of the community. The impounder or pound keeper is to give notice within twenty-four hours to the owner of the animal and ask for the owner's appearance at the impounder's residence.[74] Failure to give this notice costs the impounder fifty cents for each day's delay.[75] The owner and the impounder each appoint an appraiser to determine any damage done and if the two cannot agree they appoint a third member.[76] It is the duty of these two or three appraisers to assess the damage caused by the animal during its roaming. This figure is given to the impounder or pound keeper and, together with a fee for daily feed and care of the animal, must be paid by the owner before he regains his property.[77] Failure to pay within

---

69 *Laws of 1779*, pp. 99-101.
70 24 VSA §   871.
71 20 VSA § 3381.
72 20 VSA § 3382.
73 20 VSA § 3383.
74 20 VSA § 3413.
75 20 VSA § 3414.
76 20 VSA § 3415.
77 20 VSA § 3416.

forty-eight hours means that the impounder can advertise and sell the animal to pay his costs.[78]

If the owner of the animal is unknown, the pound keeper is to advertise the fact that the stray has been impounded, and give a description of the animal. If no one claims it within thirty days it is to be sold at public auction, after advertising the fact. The proceeds of the sale are turned over to the pound keeper who takes his fees and charges, and turns the balance, if any, over to the town treasurer. If no one has claimed the residue by the end of the year the town gets the money.[79] The laws specify the action to be taken with various kinds of animals found at large. The fees stipulated are so low that it is hard to see why anyone would want to impound a beast, except to prevent further damage, or on humanitarian grounds. However, as long as there are farmers who own livestock that may break down, push through, or jump over fences, some regulations must be provided that are not wholly extemporaneous.

K. INSPECTOR OF LUMBER, SHINGLES AND WOOD

Ever since the enactment of Chapter 8 of the *Acts of 1824*[80] permitting the selectmen to appoint a surveyor of wood and bark, the officer now called the Inspector of Lumber, Shingles, and Wood has been exercising his official duties in Vermont towns. One or more may now be appointed by the selectmen after Town Meeting.[81] These officers are to "examine and classify the quality of lumber and shingles, measure lumber, shingles and wood and give certificates thereof.[82] The work is carried out at the request of interested parties, and for his work the officer is to receive a fee of four cents a cord for the first ten cords of wood, and then one cent for each additional cord. The fee is twenty-five cents for each thousand feet of lumber measured.[83] The townspeople wanted to make certain that nobody became rich at this job.

---

78   20   VSA   §   3419.
79   20   VSA   §§   3420-3423.
80   *Laws of 1824,* p. 11.
81   24   VSA   §   871.
82   24   VSA   §   1031.
83   32   VSA   §   1676.

L. CULLER OF HOOP POLES, STAVES, AND HEADINGS

In the middle of the last century there was another town officer who worked with wood and its products — the Culler of Hoop Poles, Staves, and Headings. The town could elect one or more such cullers as it desired by vote at the Town Meeting. The function of this officer was to inspect and cull out any of the hoop poles, staves, and headings that did not come up to the exact specifications that were set in the statutes, including the number of worm holes permitted in each piece of wood.[84] It is not something new for the public to submit to regulations in the public interest, but has been present as far back as we can study the records. If it were not for the fact that times have changed and there are other methods of packaging that are more popular than barrels, we would probably still have the "cullers" with us. But fortunately, with few exceptions, as needs pass, so do the officers.

M. OTHER MINOR OFFICERS

Towns once had inspectors of flour who determined the quality of the product, following exact and detailed standards, and branded the facts on the barrels in which it was to be shipped. Penalties could be imposed on anyone who changed the inspector's marks in any way.[85] For their work the inspectors were to receive two cents for each barrel inspected and branded.[86] Somewhat the same rules applied to the inspectors of hops, who ascertained the quality of the product in the bales of hops, sealed the bale, and received twenty-five cents per bale and six cents a mile for travel to carry out their work.[87]   At the request of seven townspeople a measurer of salt was to be appointed by the selectmen. This officer received one half cent a bushel for the first 500 bushels measured and one fourth of a cent for all over 500 bushels measured at the

---

84   See *Compiled Statutes of Vermont*, 1851, p. 436.

85   *Laws of Vermont, 1824, 1825*, Chap. 57, Sec. 11, p. 462.

86   No. 28 of 1850, in *Compiled Statutes of Vermont, 1850, 1851*, p. 433.

87   *Revised Statutes of Vermont*, 1840, 1841, Chap. 68, Sections 62-65, pp. 306-361.

same time.[88]

One or more inspectors of leather were once to be elected in Town Meeting. This requirement is again one of the older sections of the statutes and can be found in *Laws of Vermont,* 1808, Vol. 1, 487-488. The officials were to inspect and stamp all leather offered for sale in the town, and for this service were to receive two cents for each piece of leather inspected. No leather could be sold, or shoes made and sold locally, unless the leather bore the official stamp that it was of the required quality. This office has long since been lost in the limbo of forgotten things. These older officers show the ever present need for protection of the public welfare. The factor of strict regulation is not new; new only are the items which the public feels need to be controlled. Changing times and conditions vary the means but not the ends of government.

Most people might be surprised to know that each town today has one or more appointed weighers of coal. They must be sworn into office and may not be connected in any way with the sale of coal. At the request of either the buyer or seller, the weigher of coal is to weigh all the coal sold in the transaction.[89] When he has performed this service he is to receive as his fee, ten cents for the first ton, and four cents for each additional one. The fee is to be paid by the person requesting the service.[90] This statute presupposes some sort of weighing device, and recalls older statutes when such instruments were neither as plentiful nor as accurate as they are today. The very first laws of Vermont required each town to procure and maintain a complete set of weights and measures of all types, linear, liquid, and weight. All measuring devices used in the town had to be checked annually against these standards and the town sets periodically compared with the state set.[91] Today the procedures for checking and testing weighing and measuring devices are handled by officials in the state Department of Agriculture.

The writer wonders if any town still has a set of these old standards of weights and measures? If there are such sets, how are they kept, and are they complete? It would appear that such a

---

88   No. 32 of *Laws of 1838,* p. 20.
89   24   VSA   §   1032.
90   32   VSA   §   1677.
91   *Laws of 1779,* pp. 400-403.

set would be of some intrinsic value, not to speak of its historical and sentimental worth. If there are no such sets around, it would seem to show that changing times have again cast off what was once useful, and that other and better, if not so picturesque, methods are now employed.

SECTION III

Special Districts

CHAPTER 20

I. Fire Districts

Over the past two decades the fastest growing form of government unit has been the special district. Originally the special district was created to perform a single function, but more recently many have been created to perform several functions and are known as multi-purpose districts. These special districts are created because existing local units cannot exercise needed services because of lack of legal authority, the political situation, or because the costs of the service would exceed the legal limits on taxation or debt totals. Frequently it has been simpler to create a new unit of government than to try to explain to or train incumbent local officials in new tasks. The most numerous of these special districts in the United States are the school districts, but they have been reduced from about 118,000 in 1942, to less than 40,000 in 1962, while other varieties of district have grown steadily in number. Some of these latter special districts have been in existence for a century and a half, while new ones are being dreamed up each year. Fortunately there is less need for new government units in Vermont where the towns have considerable latitude in their actions, as compared with other states where greater legal restrictions are imposed upon local governments.

There are, however, several types of special districts in Vermont, each filling a specific need, such as the mosquito abatement district in the Lake Dunmore area. Another form is the soil conservation district, discussed elsewhere. (pp. 137-139). The needs for conservation having been too great for the individual farmer to handle, or even for his town, it was necessary to create the larger districts based upon watershed boundaries, each of which has its own elected governing body. Here the new unit crossed existing government boundaries, to the mutual benefit of all concerned.

Another of the special purpose districts is the fire district, which formerly took in only two square miles of area in a town but which now tends to take in a larger portion of the town or even its whole area.[1] The fire district was created because under existing laws there was no provision for a town to carry on the work of fire protection as a part of its prescribed duties. The separate fire district has had a long history in Vermont. In the acts of the General Assembly in 1808, there are special acts incorporating a Middlebury Fire Society,[2] and a Burlington Fire Company,[3] while in 1809, Montpelier was so favored.[4] These special acts were worded in almost the same terms and provided for the same powers and duties as are found in the present day statutes.[5]

Present day fire districts are of two types, either a portion of the town to be determined by those who desire fire protection, or, of the entire town. In the first instance the district is created by the selectmen upon the written petition of twenty freeholders of the proposed district. The selectmen are to fix the boundaries of the district and record them in the office of the town clerk.[6] The selectmen then issue the warning for the first meeting, at which the first selectman, or in his absence, either of the other two, presides. The meeting may vote to create the district or to reject the proposal. When the people vote to create the fire district they elect the required officers and are an existing entity. The annual meeting of the fire district is held on the second Monday in January, with as many necessary special meetings as may be called, all of them on six days' notice.[7] At the annual meeting, the fire district elects a clerk, a treasurer, a collector of taxes, and a member of the prudential committee. The prudential committee serves in the same capacity as the town selectmen and their terms and method of election are also the same. The fire district may also elect a chief engineer and as many assistant engineers as are felt to be needed; the latter

---

1 Since 1951, No. 77 of the *Acts of 1951*.
2 *Laws of 1808*, p. 42.
3 *Ibid*. p. 157.
4 *Laws of 1809*, p. 110.
5 See 20 VSA Chapter 171.
6 20 VSA § 2481.
7 20 VSA § 2483.

are to rank in the order of their election.[8]

In the second case, when the whole town is to be the fire district, the same steps as outlined above are followed, except that it takes a majority vote of three-fourths of those present and voting to organize the district.[9] The same officers are elected for the town fire district,[10] except that the fire district may vote to have the town selectmen serve as the governing body.[11] The town tax collector may serve as the tax collector for either form of fire district when each so votes,[12] and when this happens, his duties are the same as for the town. The fire district may levy and collect taxes for its own purposes, and in the process the prudential committee and tax collectors have all the duties and rights that the similar town officers have.[13] If any fire districts vote to do so, they may adopt the town manager system for the exercise of their work.

In their functions and purposes fire districts prove very interesting. They may protect the property within their boundaries from damage by fire by buying and maintaining the proper equipment.[14] They may construct and maintain sewers, sewage treatment works, sidewalks, public parks, and public lighting systems, as well as any other lawful purpose.[15] By vote any fire district may cause its streets to be sprinkled or oiled.[16] In other words, the fire district in Vermont has become a sort of catch-all for performing a variety of functions that the towns, as such, are unable or unwilling to perform under ordinary circumstances. To this extent the name "fire district" is somewhat a misnomer, but since the main reason for organizing the bulk of the districts in the first place was fire protection, the name is probably the best that could be applied.

Every year the daily press reports on a larger number of fires in Vermont with consequent heavy losses. It is obvious that not enough towns take advantage of the statutes permitting creation of

---

8	20	VSA	§	2485.
9	20	VSA	§	2541.
10	20	VSA	§	2542.
11	20	VSA	§	2543.
12	20	VSA	§	2486.
13	20	VSA	§	2601.
14	20	VSA	§	2543.
15	20	VSA	§	2601.
16	20	VSA	§	2603.

a fire district. A great many fires are reported to have their origin in defective electrical wiring and to reduce this hazard more towns should appoint a wiring inspector, as is authorized in the statutes.[17] Better yet would be to have the fire districts vote by-laws that provide for proper inspection of all property by the chief engineer or his assistant. Such action is legally authorized by statute.[18] When there is actually a fire, the chief engineer or the assistant of highest rank present, has complete charge of the firefighting,[19] including the right to call for aid from the bystanders and the right to penalize for refusal. Adding inspection duties to the work of these men would appear to be a wise precaution, for it would permit them to know more about local property and potential fire hazards.

17 24 VSA § 1033.
18   5 VSA § 2602.
19 20 VSA § 2673.

CHAPTER 21

II. Soil Conservation Districts

An important factor in the abandonment of farms and the consequent loss of population is the loss of cultivable soil — a problem which plagues all states. For over three hundred years the people who settled and cultivated the land in this nation have been profligate with their most precious resource — the soil. As a consequence for years and perhaps for centuries, millions of acres of land can not be used for cultivation. Other millions of acres, greatly injured by mal-practice, produce only a portion of what they should.

Fortunately, new ideas of conservation appeared and over the past quarter of a century efforts have been made to remedy the losses and to prevent future soil depletion. The work is a joint project of the federal government, the states, and individual farmers and landowners. These projects began in 1935, when the federal Department of Agriculture was authorized to set up soil conservation programs which had for their main purpose the alleviation of the distressed situation of agriculture, distress greatly worsened by the current great Depression. In attempting to carry out the mandate of Congress a draft soil conservation law was drawn up and circulated among the states. One by one all of the states adopted the proposed law, or a variation of it.

Vermont did not escape the consequences of improper farming practices and her hills and valleys showed what happens when rules of good cultivation are not followed. As the thin skin of soil was washed away, the stony acres that remained could not provide an adequate living for the landowners. Farms were abandoned and towns declined in population as the citizens escaped to new homes where grinding toil was not a prerequisite for life. As time went on, the process of erosion and soil loss increased in tempo and there was a real danger that nothing but barren stone piles would remain.

Vermont took the first steps in the soil conservation program in 1939, when the General Assembly enacted a law providing for the creation of a State Soil Conservation Committee and the establishment of local soil conservation districts. This first law was without enforcement teeth and consequently no action was under way by the time the next session of the General Assembly convened in 1941. Having seen the light, the legislators amended the statute, enacting the enforcement features which they had refused to accept two years before. The new law gave soil conservation districts the status of governmental units, but they were nowhere given the power to levy taxes.[20] A soil conservation district was to be created by the state committee following an affirmative vote in an election held under its supervision.[21] The state committee had to call an election when twenty-five landowners, of one or more acres in the proposed district, petitioned for its creation.[22]

Acting under the authority of the statute, thirteen soil conservation districts, covering the entire state, were organized by the summer of 1947. Every district was created as the result of an overwhelmingly favorable vote of the individual landowners residing within the proposed district. Once created each district sets up its own rules and regulations, and under specified conditions, may increase, divide, combine, or abolish its area and existence.[23] None of the districts have been self-supporting. To make the programs possible small sums have been secured from state appropriations, and much larger grants from the national government.

These districts have been very effective and have brought about major changes in agricultural practices. Watershed areas have been reforested, streams have been straightened, and new banks protected against erosion. Land has been terraced, strip farming has been carried on, drainage projects have been completed, and proper land use has been illustrated and has consequently been stimulated.

---

20 10 VSA § 415; see also the Annotation to 10 VSA § 402 which says statutes grant powers to local supervisors; *1950 Opinions Attorney General* 227.

21 10 VSA §§ 412, 413.

22 10 VSA § 402; 10 VSA §§ 409, 410.

23 10 VSA §§ 417, 429, 436-440.

Some of the districts embrace portions of different counties, and all include many towns. Local boundaries have been disregarded in order to creater larger areas; by pooling their resources and by working cooperatively on problems that transcend local boundaries the individual farmers and the districts as a whole have succeeded in bringing about conditions otherwise impossible. Each improvement has made further cooperation simpler.

It is not necessary to discuss the other special districts of limited application in a general work of this nature, but the major special district, the school district, should be described, and to that subject it is now necessary to turn.

CHAPTER 22

III. School Districts

In a free society one of the most important of all the functions of government is to provide a school system for the education of the youth of that society. In Vermont, this function has been performed primarily by the towns and cities, and today is supervised by a State Board of Education and the State Department of Education. The state itself has always taken an interest in education, and following the lead of the Wentworth charters, each town charter granted by the General Assembly provided that one or more lots in the town were to be reserved for the use of the schools. The first *Constitution of 1777* provided that ". . . a competent number of schools ought to be maintained in each town . . ."[1] In order to get around the words "in each town" so that consolidation of town school districts would be possible, the Constitution was amended in 1955, by adding the clause "or by towns jointly with the consent of the General Assembly."[2]

In the October 1782, session of the General Assembly that body enacted the first legislation to augment the constitutional statement pertaining to education. The law said that each town which needed more than one school to accommodate its needs could create as many new school districts as it desired at any legal meeting, and could "alter the same from time to time."[3] By 1797, it was decreed that the children of school age in a town were those persons from four to eighteen years af age, and that a list of such students was to be compiled annually.[4]

---

1 *Vermont Consttiution, 1777*, Chapter II, Sec. XL, and in the current Constitution, Chapter II, Sec. 64.
2 No. 190, *Acts of 1953*, pp. 170-171.
3 *Laws of 1782*, p. 22.
4 *Laws of Vermont*, 1797, Chap. LIV, p. 497.

By 1797, also, it was discovered that the first laws did not cover all cases where the town "cannot conveniently be accommodated with school . . ." and a change was made to permit any three or more of the inhabitants to petition the selectmen for the organization of a new school district.[5] The selectmen were then to call a meeting for the proposed district and one of them was to preside until a clerk and other officers were elected.[6] This procedure could go on indefinitely as petty squabbles and local jealousies rent the towns, so that some towns had twenty-five or more minute school districts. The writer once saw an Atlas of 1877 that showed twenty-five school districts in a certain town. Each was numbered seratim, and each had its own school house and consequently, its own set of officers. In 1890, the top figure for a town was twenty-one school districts.[7] It is interesting to note that this proliferation of school districts came from a misinterpretation of the original acts. These were based, not upon a love of one room schools, but upon the determination of the early inhabitants that adequate instruction would be furnished to the students. While a portion of the increase in schools could be ascribed to an increase in the population, most of it was due to the internecine conflict in the towns.

By the 1850's the decline in the population of many towns was so great the towns found it increasingly difficult to support the excessive number of schools. People began to grumble and by 1865, agitation for town school districts appeared in many places.[8] By 1870, the General Assembly had made it possible for towns voluntarily to abolish the numerous districts and create one town school district.[9] In the next twenty years some forty towns took the step, but fifteen of them rescinded the action later.[10] The pressure for reduction in the number of districts continued, and by virtue of what must have been astute parliamentary maneuvering, the General As-

---

5 *Laws of Vermont*, 1797, Chap. LIV, p. 494.

6 *Ibid.*

7 *The Thirty-Second Vermont School Report, Montpelier, 1892*, pp. 85-157.

8 Mason Stone, *History of Education, State of Vermont, 1777-1927*, Montpelier, no date, but probably 1929, p. 59.

9 No. 10 of the *Acts of 1870*, pp. 38 ff.

10 Stone, *op. cit.*, p. 59.

sembly in 1892 abolished the old districts and created town school districts as of July 1893.[11] In 1890 there had been 2,214 school districts and 2,424 schools. The sudden loss of nearly two thousand school districts at one swoop has been held to be a real crime by certain older persons with whom the writer has talked. To maintain the entity of their former districts some thirty independent or incorporated districts were soon created, and although many disappeared, new ones were formed and nineteen still exist today,[13] and with the town districts now comprise a total of 263, or a little more than one-tenth of the number seventy years ago.

Many factors helped create the former chaotic school situation — among them the impassability of the roads for many months in the winter, and the need for short school years so the labor of children could be utilized in making a living on the farms of the state. These conditions no longer exist. There is an excellent network of good roads that are open the year around, except for short periods after heavy snow storms. The labor of children is no longer used on farms as it once was — machines and paid labor have taken its place, and finally, outside of a few larger towns, the loss of population has been such that there are no longer enough children to fill the school houses. Because of all this, one can only echo the words of a student of local government when he said, ". . . so far as one can measure such things, education has progressed in rough proportion to the abandonment of the district plan of organization."[14]

It is necessary to return again to the discussion of local school districts as functioning legal entities. Under the early laws each district was to levy and collect taxes for the support of its school; the charge was a lien upon its property. In the laws of 1797, the property of non-resident owners was exempt from these tax charges.[15] This situation remained until by an act of the General Assembly on November 7, 1818, this exemption was removed and all property was treated alike.[16] In 1810, the towns were required

---

11   No. 20 of the *Acts of 1892*, pp. 24 ff.
12   *The Thirty-Second Vermont School Report, op cit.*
13   *Vermont Educational Directory*, 1962 - 1963, pp. 15 - 18.
14   Lane Lancaster, *Government in Rural America*, New York, 1937, p. 274.
15   *Laws of Vermont, 1797*, Chapter LIV, pp. 495 and 497.
16   *Laws of 1818*, October Session, p. 84.

to levy a one cent tax on the grand list, whose returns were to be deposited in the town treasury.[17] The figure was set at two cents in 1824,[18] and shortly after that the levying of taxes was made uniform with other aspects of local government. The product of the two cent tax was to be paid out to the school districts in the town which had maintained a school for two months in the year, and in proportion to the children from four to eighteen years of age who resided in the district.[19].

Each district was to spend its money under the supervision of a prudential committee which was elected annually.[20] The committee had charge of all the affairs of the district, including the construction or rental of a building, its equipment, and maintenance,[21] as well as the hiring of the teacher.[22] It also appears that at one time the prudential committee licensed its own teachers. Except for the last item, this general pattern is still followed in town school districts, which since the Act of 1893, have superceded the local districts described above; in the nineteen incorporated districts; and in the six operating union districts. This is a total of 263. The union district idea is not a new one, because in 1808, the General Assembly provided that any number of persons from two or more towns could petition their selectmen for a combined district which would include land from the different towns.[23] As the writer reads the law this was an early forerunner of modern school consolidation.

Today, each town and incorporated school district holds an annual meeting — the former is frequently held at the same time as the Town Meeting.[24] The school meeting is warned by the selectmen in the same manner and usually in the same document as the Town Meeting, and when met serves as the chief policy making body for the district. One school director is elected annually for a three year tearm,[25] and the three school directors are now charged

17 *Laws of 1810*, Chapter 107, p. 150.
18 *Laws of 1824*, Chapter 7, p. 10.
19 *Laws of 1810*, p. 154.
20 *Laws of Vermont*, 1797, p. 494, Sec. 2.
21 *Ibid.*, p. 498, Sec. 9.
22 *Ibid.*, p. 493, Sec. 9.
23 *Laws of Vermont, 1808*, Chapter 41, p. 54.
24 16 VSA § 362.
25 16 VSA § 381.

with the responsibility of maintaining the school facilities of the town. Since 1961, the following restriction applies to the election of a school director. "A custodian, teacher, principal or superintendent of a town school district acting as such shall not be eligible to hold office as a member of the local board of the town where he is employed."[26] The law also provides that the town may elect one or two additional school directors for a one year term at a time, only. The term expires on the next Town Meeting day after the election.[27] The directors are trustees for the district funds, and are liable for any wrongful expenditures. The directors are required to make an annual report by July 15, to the State Department of Education on the amount of money spent and other information as requested by the department. Unless this is done, the town will not receive any of the school funds which are given to the towns by the state.[29].

The directors must also report to the town in the annual Town Report in the same manner,[30] and in addition show what has been spent between the preceding July 1, and the end of the town fiscal year. They must also show what they propose to spend for the rest of the time until June 30, and how much they will need for the next year. All this includes items about the total number of students, total number of days of school, and average daily attendance. The directors propose a sum to be spent and the district votes a specific tax rate on the grand list for current expenses — for any deficit, for capital improvements, and for any other lawful expenditures.[31] All this has to be carefully planned, for unless the town votes enough money, which, when added to the proposed state aid money, totals $130 per pupil, the state will refuse to pay the state aid and the town will be left with a deficit of about half its total school costs, or more.[32]

---

26 16 VSA § 381, as amended by No. 91 of the *Acts of 1961*, p. 73.
27 16 VSA § 381.
28 16 VSA § 386.
29 16 VSA § 388.
30 16 VSA § 389.
31 16 VSA § 3222.
32 16 VSA § 3444 (a).

The annual district meeting does not need to elect a clerk or treasurer because these two town officers ex officio serve in the same posts in the town school district.[33] An incorporated school district at its annual meeting elects a clerk and treasurer from among the legal voters of the district[34] and may elect the town collector the district tax collector.[35] All these officers, including the prudential committee, act in their official capacities as do their counterpart officers in the town school district.[36] In union school districts the officers are elected according to different regulations;[37] but their duties, powers, and liabilities are the same as those of all other school directors.[38]

A. SCHOOL CONSOLIDATION

In all the fifty states of this nation there is the real problem of how to support the schools of those states. One answer has been to consolidate districts and improve both the financial base and the quality of the education program. In 1942, there were 116,000 school districts in the existing forty-eight states. By the end of 1962, there seems to have been a total of about 37,000 with a definite tendency to continue the rapid reduction in numbers. Vermont made its great reduction in 1893, but since then has done very little along that line. Although the early legislatures showed a willingness to permit such consolidation recent legislatures have tended to drag their feet and to put as many roadblocks in the path to consolidation as possible. There have been laws permitting some kind of unification of districts since 1945, but only since 1953, have they been effective. The handicaps to consolidation have been difficult to overcome, even though the step is wholly optional. In 1963, sixteen union districts had been set up, but only six were operating. Two had been dissolved by legislative action, and eight were in the process of organizing, or were delayed by one or more towns chang-

33 16 VSA §§ 411 and 3223.
34 16 VSA §   491.
35 16 VSA §   494.
36 16 VSA §   497.
37 16 VSA §   613.
38 16 VSA §   616.

ing their original vote. In the face of a national trend this is not a very productive record.

All kinds of arguments are presented against the trend, but most of them are really excuses. The real question is, "Are the children of Vermont getting an education designed to equip them to face the problems of living in an atomic age?" It is here alone that debate is really valid. There was a time, when the whole country was using the "little red school house" almost exclusively, that such schools were considered suitable and truly seemed to be. But today, in all progressive states and areas of states, there is a trend away from the little one or two room schools to larger schools which are better equipped and more adequately staffed. In such schools competition is keener, facilities are better, and more adequate programs can be offered. It usually costs proportionately less to give more services in these schools because more people are cooperating in their support. Many people feel that school consolidation is a major answer if Vermont is to keep on a competitive basis in educational standards.

The opposition to such proposals points out the rising costs of schools, the closing of roads by winter snows, (probably with tongue in cheek), the need for children to wait by the roadside in stormy weather, the long hours away from home, and a thousand and one other logical reasons, as well as a host of excuses used to prevent calm discussion of the real facts in the case. Then, there are those wearing rosy bifocals, who argue for a glorious golden past which exists in the nostalgic recesses of their minds, largely because they didn't live when life was hard and conditions were really primitive. Few of the opponents to consolidation discuss the position of Vermont in relation to other states in the Union. The average advantages of children throughout the nation with respect to their schools is most important, for the country rises or falls according to its ability to transmit its information on to the next generation on a qualitative basis. Since the country is made up of all its parts, the position of Vermont is as important as any other state.

If Vermont schools are not as good, or better, than those of other states, our young people will pay for our neglect in the loss of competitive positions in the world in which they find themselves. The question of relative educational position has been given a great deal of thought in this country, and even before World War II was causing much concern. In 1938, an excellent *Report of the Advisory Committee on Education,* reporting to the President of the United States, said:

"Education can be made a force to equalize the condition of men. It is no less true that it may be a force to create class, race and sectional distinctions. The evidence indicates clearly that the schools of the United States, which have hitherto been regarded as the bulwark of democracy, may in fact become an instrument for creating those very inequalities they were designed to prevent. If, for a long period of years, each succeeding generation is drawn in disproportionately large numbers from those areas in which economic conditions are poorest, if the population reserves of the nation continue to be recruited from economically underprivileged groups, and if the inability of the depressed economic areas and groups to provide proper education for their children is not corrected by aid from areas and groups more prosperous, the effect on American civilization and on representative political institutions may be disastrous."

The prophetic implication of this extract can be seen in the current racial and economic strife in this country where the major pressure emenates from those groups to whom opportunities have not been available. The consequences and costs of these backward policies have not yet been cast.

There is the same validity for these ideas in Vermont as there is in the nation. It is a well known fact that the largest increase of population proportionately came from the areas which were poorest in terms of resources. Thus, in order to support a poor quality school, the poorest areas of this state, and of the nation as well, have been forced to pay out a much larger proportion of their smaller tax total to support their schools than have the wealthier areas. In spite of all their efforts they got an inferior product. It is for this reason that the grant-in-aid program has evolved. The more prosperous areas help support the poorest sections in order that the state or nation as a whole may have a better average condition for whatever activity the funds are used. But if the grant fails to get the results sought because the recipient is not efficient, then the help is wasted and the general level is reduced and not raised as intended, for the wealthier areas could have made good use of that which was taken from them. It is here that the problem of existing schools versus union schools needs a close scrutiny because of the limited funds available.

B. SCHOOL FINANCES

Vermont is neither the richest nor the poorest state, per capita, in the Union and her schools tend to bear out this fact. The state has not been able to reach the average support figure as found for the country as a whole. In 1943-44, the federal statistics showed that the state of Vermont paid only 14 per cent of the total cost of its public schools, as opposed to a national average of 33 per cent paid by all state governments. At the same time Vermont towns paid 84.4 per cent of the total costs of their schools as compared with a national average of only 60 per cent. These figures included less enlightened states like Georgia and Mississippi. In 1962, the state of Vermont paid 20 per cent of the total school costs while the national average was 40 per cent.[39] At the same time, the towns now pay between fifty and sixty per cent of their total town budgets on school costs, and find that even with this exertion they have second rate schools. There are 83 high schools in Vermont and only 64 of them have more than 100 students as a total enrollment. In fact, the average attendance for the ten smallest high schools is less than 60 pupils. These figures are disheartening from the standpoint of an adequate educational program. The question of school support in Vermont is a pressing one because of the small population and limited resources. Careful planning, intelligent economy, and better understanding of school problems will be needed if money resources of the state are not to be strained beyond endurance.

Already state educational costs are growing at rates that raise questions for the future. For fiscal year 1948, the General Assembly appropriated the sum of $3,206,805.00 for all educational purposes from the elementary schools through the university level. In fiscal year 1962, the comparative figure was $22,952,882.50 with only $15,987,115.12 actually spent. This is a fivefold increase in the fourteen years. The same relative figures are found for grants-

---

39   The cost figures are found in *State Board of Education, Biennial Report, 1962*, p. 22.

in-aid to the town. In fiscal year 1948, the state granted $1,984,-070.42 to the towns, while in the fiscal year 1962, the figures are $5,476,579.23 plus $685,813.24 for aid in school building construction. If the towns of Vermont had to add these sums to their burdens the tax load in many towns would become lethal.

The complaints about costs are legitimate, but modern life does take more money than in the past. Also, when the government spends only about fifty per cent more for the education of its citizens than its constituents do to satiate their physical appetites to the extent of a nearly $10,000,000 alcoholic beverage business, it cannot be said that all has been done that might be done to solve its fiscal problems.

C. SCHOOL TRANSPORTATION

Another example of changing needs is the necessity for transporting children from their homes to the schoolhouse. When there were 2,400 schools in the state even young children could walk the mile or so to school. Today when there may be only one or two schools in a town, the distance involved may be several miles, and with high speed automobiles whizzing by, the child is in real danger. When more effective schools are provided in union districts, the distances and dangers are augmented. Hence the need for a program of school buses.

Vermont law permits the school directors to provide for transporting students to schools within their jurisdiction.[40] Some provision for school transportation has been found in state law ever since 1876, when arrangements could be made for the same.[41] Since 1947, the directors can buy and operate their own buses. As the law seems to read, it prohibits the transportation of high school students.[42] It is not clear whether this is permissible, even though it is being done, either with or without a vote of the town. If the law can be interpreted so as to deny pupils of high school age the privilege of being transported to school, it would appear to be a

---

40 16 VSA §§ 1221-1224.
41 No. 45 of the *Acts of 1876*.
42 16 VSA § 1223.

grave discrimination against children who live in the many towns without high schools.

Problems here are the same throughout the United States. Transportation regulations often prohibit the picking-up of children closer to the school than a prescribed distance, deny the privilege to those over a fixed age, etc. The regulations are made in an earnest effort to permit the schools to do an adequate job, yet none of the attempts have proved to be wholly satisfactory.

In the past, almost anyone could carry children to school and did. The writer has seen a makeshift body on a small truck that served the purpose of transporting children to and from school, and did double-duty the rest of the day carrying garbage from the city to feed the owner's hogs. Even so, this vehicle was sturdier than many school buses that formerly were seen. Fortunately this is a matter of ancient history. Over a decade ago Representative Reid Lefevre led a valiant battle in the General Assembly to require adequate standards for vehicles used in transporting children. He was successful and today one no longer holds one's breath when a rattling bus goes by. All must be properly equipped and inspected.[43] Every bus must carry liability insurance of prescribed sums and be able to prove it at all time.[44] Unfortunately the law seems to exempt the individual who drives his own children to school, with or without pay.

It is a tribute to the care and devotion of the bus drivers, both before and since the enactment of the regulations, that there have been no major accidents in Vermont, even though driving conditions can be extremely hazardous at times. School buses generally are well maintained and keep rigid schedules so that there is little need for children to wait out in the weather. School transportation has become an accepted part, albeit an expensive one, of the school system, and except where lack of finances means too few buses and consequently earlier home-leaving and later home-returning times, is an accepted part of the town scene.

D.   TEACHING STAFF AND SALARIES

As important as matters previously discussed in this chapter

---

43   23   VSA   §§   1281, 1282.
44   23   VSA   §   921.

may be, none of them are relevant without teachers to lead the students in their studies. Neither new buildings nor bright, shiny school buses have significance if there is no instruction. Here is where many plans have gone astray, because there simply were not enough competent teachers available to meet the demand. With the long tradition of education in this country, the phenomenon needs some explanation.

There are a variety of factors involved, but they are not always the same for any two places. Hence the one we mention here is that it is generally agreed that teachers are not paid enough for their work. The kind of education which young people get will determine the future growth and development of the nation. Yet many people have been willing to relegate this important function to persons inadequately trained for their work, or who, when trained, have no assurance of being able to continue in their field because citizens have refused to believe that the average teacher is entitled to more than a subsistence wage.

As recently as 1941-1942, federal statistics showed that the average teacher's salary was only $1,001 a year. The average for urban teachers was $1,395, and for rural teachers $843 per year. When it is remembered that these figures are all averages, it is easy to see that there were many indeed who received less than these amounts. In 1945, the General Assembly of Vermont increased the minimum pay to $1,000 per year and in 1947, the minimum was fixed at $1,500 per year for one year of training. The minimum for two year's training was $1,600, $1,700 for three, and $1,800 for four years of training. In 1962, the figures were respectively $2,700, $3,100, $3,400 and $3,700.[45] A teacher without a professional certificate has a minimum salary of $2,500 per year.[46] These figures are substantially below averages in other states, but are much better than they were. When the teacher has completed ten years of teaching the minimum figures are raised to $3,800, $4,200, $4,500 and $4,800 for one, two, three, or four years of college preparation.

The original pay increases in the 1940's were designed to keep as many trained teachers in the state as possible. Unfortunately, some towns proceeded to discharge their experienced and trained

---

45   16   VSA   §   1792.
46   16   VSA   §   1791.

teachers in order to hire new ones at the lowest pay level. Children in those towns really were to be pitied because little consideration was given to them, only to the pocketbooks of their parents. It is the frame of mind which makes "savings" of this nature possible which has really injured the teaching profession. Too often the teacher with ideas and ability has been so oppressed by the negative viewpoint of the school district and its penny-pinchers that he or she has left in disgust. Also, too often the patrons of a school expect a double standard of action and morals; the school teacher is supposed to act like a non-feeling automaton, the townspeople to act without restraint and "doing what comes naturally." This hypocrisy has driven many good teachers from the field.

No amount of money put into scholarships, nor pious exhortations about service, will increase the number of students entering teacher training programs unless the prospective teachers can be assured of different treatment in their careers than has been accorded to teachers in the past. The continuing shortage of teaching personnel is mostly chargeable to general public opinion, and to low income. For a long time Vermont, and some other states as well, has had far too great an overturn in its educational staff. It is estimated that there should be a normal turnover of about four per cent of the total number of teachers per year. Just before World War II the rate in Vermont was slightly over nine per cent, or more than double what it should have been. In 1963, the rate was 13.5 per cent.

Similar conditions in all parts of the country caused an expert in the field of local government to offer the following comment about teaching: "It is silly to speak of elementary teaching as a profession under conditions which automatically exclude men with families and turn over the instruction of our children immature girls prone to look upon this employment as a mere stopgap."[47] This will continue to be true as long as unskilled labor can receive more than trained teachers — a situation often only too true.

The same writer has also said, "The fact that some millions of our rural children are instructed by immature, poorly-prepared, inexperienced female nomads, uninterested in their work or in the

---

47 Lane Lancaster, *Government in Rural America*, New York, 1937, p. 292.

communities which they serve, is directly traceable to the attitude of the public which employs them and which exacts from them a stultifying conformity to a set of mores admirably calculated to drive from the work the ambitious, the energetic, the intellectually honest, in fact, any who care to preserve a sense of personal dignity."[48] The foregoing statement is less applicable today than in 1937, for there are more economic opportunities available to young women, and they tend to shun the teaching profession. At the same time older women, whose children are no longer a confining care, are turning to the profession, and since they have their roots in the community, the "nomadism" mentioned above, is no longer the factor it was earlier.

Vermont has had as many as a fourth of its teachers with only temporary and emergency certificates and still finds it necessary to use far too many such today. Unless we can attract and keep adequately trained and experienced teachers we cannot raise our standards from mediocre to good, or best, and without that, our leading export, the young people of the state, will be handicapped in their competition for a livelihood. Since much of our problem is money, careful consideration of economies, and efficiencies in school consolidation, should be the first steps in plans for the future.

48   Lancaster, *Ibid.*, p. 294-295.

The Suffrage and Representation

CHAPTER 23

Voting Requirements

The citizens of the towns of Vermont are called upon to participate in one or more elections every year. These include the Town Meeting, primary elections, special elections, and the general elections in the fall of the even years. Were there not some restrictions placed upon the exercise of this act of civic responsibility there would be real possibilities of improper voting. As it is, the law prescribes so many safeguards that upon a casual reading of the law there seems to be slight chance of citizen participation in the voting. Further study shows these impediments to be more apparent than real.

"Every citizen twenty-one years of age or more, having resided in the state one year next preceding a general election, who has taken the Freeman's Oath as provided in the constitution,"[1] may vote for his choices in the general election in the town where he resides. There is the further stipulation that he must have resided in the town of his residence on the day of election for a period of three months.[2] The full right of males to vote has been granted since the *Constiution of 1777,* was written, and that of females since the 19th Amendment was adopted in Vermont in 1924.[3]

There have always been requirements to be fulfilled before voting in Vermont. The oldest of these is the taking of the Freeman's Oath, which must be taken before a town official after the board of civil authority in a town has given its "approbation."[4] The oath requires a person always to vote as in his conscience seems

---

1 17 VSA § 62.
2 *Ibid.*
3 *Constitution of Vermont,* Chapter II, Section 34.
4 17 VSA § 68, See also XVI *Vermont Quarterly* (New Series), No. 2, April 1948, Andrew E. Nuquist, "Freeman's Oath," pp. 53-64.

best, without fear or favor of any man. The observance of this oath through the years has kept the elections in Vermont on a high plane.

In addition to the requirements of United States citizenship,[5] Vermont citizenship as shown by residence in the state,[6] and local residence as shown by the place where a person has his home, there is the additional stipulation that before exercising the privilege of voting in Town Meeting the person must be listed by the board of listers in his town as having paid his taxes on that list. This is the poll tax payment that has long caused debate. The poll tax was discussed earlier in this study.[7]

For nearly three quarters of a century of the state's history there seems to have been no formal method of keeping track of the legal voters in the towns. Local knowledge of the person's residence in the town was enough to guarantee the integrity of the ballot. However, for some reason not easily discovered today, the General Assembly in the session of 1866, made provision for the creation of a "check list" of the eligible voters.[8] The list was to be drawn up by the selectmen at the request of ten per cent of the voters in the last election. These persons were required to submit a written petition over their signatures. The law was amended in 1867, so that the selectmen were given the mandatory duty of making up the list in every town with more than 500 votes.[9] In 1870, the law was again changed so that twenty or more persons had to petition for the list in town with fewer than 4,000 citizens. In all towns with more than 4,000 citizens the list was mandatory. In both cases the selectmen were required to act thirty days before the election.[10] After a series of minor changes and revisions the General Assembly of 1915, enacted the law that is essentially the one still in use.[11] This provided for a separate check list for the general election and for Town Meeting, each to be drawn up especially for each election, with the exception of special congressional elections, when the list for the last general election is to be used.

---

5   17   VSA   §   61.
6   17   VSA   §   62.
7   See pp. 51-54.
8   No. 15 of the *Acts of 1866*, p. 19.
9   No. 24 of the *Acts of 1867*, pp. 31-33.
10   No. 86 of the *Acts of 1870*, pp. 125, 126.
11   No. 1 of the *Acts of 1915*, p. 3.

The law still prescribes that the selectmen make the check list of legal voters. They must make an alphabetical list of the voters thirty days before a general election,[12] and an alphabetical list of the qualified voters in Town Meeting twelve and not more than twenty days before the meeting.[13] In both instances, they must post notices in two or more public places in the town and leave a copy with the town clerk.

While the check list for general elections should include every person over twenty-one years of age, resident in the state for one year, and in the town for three months, and who has taken the Freeman's Oath,[14] the check list for Town Meeting is more restricted. Since No. 111 of the *Acts of 1915*, the law has been that there is the additional requirement of having his "list including poll," taken at the last annual assessment preceding the meeting, or on having reached the age of twenty-one since that time. Poll taxes have to be paid by January first, or the individual may not vote in Town Meeting.[15] This stipulation has caused some trouble in recent years because many persons still remember when the prescribed date was February first.

In taking the list of polls the law now prescribes a long list of exemptions for persons who shall be placed in the list with the words "poll exempt" placed after their names, together with their respective classification.[16] Some towns have made the mistake of preventing these persons from voting in Town Meeting, which is entirely wrong. Section 701 of Title 24, VSA states that anyone otherwise eligible "who is exempt from taxation for any cause, shall be a voter in Town Meeting while residing in such town." Exemption, and non-payment, are two entirely different things in the eyes of the law, and exemption no more deprives a person of his vote than does the fact that he is tall or short.

Since there are these two check lists to be prepared there is a major weakness that should be repaired. The check list used in the Town Meeting is a more restricted list, and is usually used in pre-

---

12 17 VSA §   201.
13 17 VSA §   241.
14 17 VSA §   62.
15 24 VSA §   701.
16 32 VSA § 3801.

paring the check list for the primary and general elections. When the ordinary poll taxpayer protests, he is forced to pay his poll tax to vote in the general election, a requirement which is not legal. This is a generally accepted method of exerting pressure. The law should be clearly stated so that the check list of the previous general election, as amended and changed by the prescribed legal means, be used in the fall elections ,and not the restricted spring list, in order to prevent extra legal voting requirements from appearing. Voting should be free in fact, as it has been in law since 1777.

CHAPTER 24

The Australian Ballot

The chief purpose for townspeople coming together in Town Meeting is to cast a vote for town officers, or for some proposal for action. There is need for a decision, and here it is made by a counting of heads. If no decision is reached the meeting will have been to no purpose. It is the free expression of opinions followed by a non-coercive vote which sets democratic forms of government apart from the totalitarian dictatorships. Any weakening of the method of getting a true expression of public sentiment is thus a blow against self-government.

The origin and historical development of the Town Meeting shows that it was to be used as a sounding board for the expression of opinion. Every question was to be raised, discussed, criticised, torn apart, rebuilt, and finally accepted or rejected by the people present. The free expression of all viewpoints was held to be the best guarantee that hasty or ill-advised action would be prevented. Under this system it was often true that the town talker would monopolize the floor so long that an early vote was taken as the only method of silencing the flood of words. But even this was not without its value, for the tolerant citizens would be silently marshalling all the arguments on the other side, so that the speaker was really the best argument for the opposition. The truth of this aspect of the procedure was really felt, if not always understood in the towns of Vermont, and is something almost incomprehensible to those who have not grown up in an atmosphere of self-government.

It was true that many who attended Town Meeting were not in sympathy with the wordiness of some of the participants and resented having to listen to all the talk. As the years went on, those who felt this way gradually came to be a majority in many towns.

It is unfortunate that this was so, for when intelligent and interested discussion dies out, self-government gives way to supervision. To quiet the criticisms of these people, the General Assembly made it possible to use the Australian ballot in Town Meeting,[17] which meant voting without discussion.

When used in the general elections, the Australian ballot helps to preserve the purity of the suffrage. The ballots are printed and distributed at public expense, and must be marked in secret. In most states where it is used the Australian ballot is cast by the person who marks it and places it in the ballot box himself, but in Vermont, it is given to persons presiding at the ballot boxes, a few of whom occasionally violate the principle of secrecy by managing to look at the markings before they place the ballot in the box. Fortunately, this is rarely done, or the state would be in the clutches of machines as corrupt as those of some of the well-known city bosses.

Thus, while the use of the Australian ballot in general elections is wise, it is another matter to use it in Town Meeting. It's use destroys the chief characteristic of the gathering, the necessity for everyone interested to be there to vote in person on specific issues. Under the older practice of voting, people came because they were afraid they would lose their vote on some important officer or issue. Today, in those towns using the Australian ballot, when a person can come in at any time after the opening of the polls and prior to their closing, and spend five minutes in marking and casting his ballot, he has not participated in discussion on the subjects, and often does not know the issues involved. His voting thus loses much of its value. Just voting itself is not very valuable; the citizen must vote *for* or *against* something, and this cannot be done unless the factors involved are understood. There is general criticism that the use of the Australian ballot has reduced interest in town meeting and resulted in less competent voting.

Probably some sort of study should be made to determine the effect of the Australian ballot on the government of Vermont towns by reducing the necessity for attendance. Any proposal to remove the Australian ballot from the Town Meeting raises the point that this would be unfair because many, who could not afford to give up

---

17   No. 1 of *Acts of 1892*, p. 3;   No. 3 of *Acts of 1894*, and now found as 24 VSA § 726.

a day's pay to stay at the meeting, would be deprived of a vote. There is some merit to this contention, and perhaps it could be answered by making the first Tuesday in March a legal holiday in Vermont. There would then be little or no reason for non-attendance.

The argument may be raised that the decisions on how people are going to vote are not made in the meeting anyway, but are arrived at before the meeting convenes. But deciding matters in secret, or in rump sessions, is not the democratic way of self-government; a ballot cast on this basis, or on no information at all, is not one of much value. There seem to be few reasons advanced by those who favor the Australian ballot, save those of expediency, while there are good reasons for voting in Town Meeting only after full discussion. It is a weakness to have more people come in to cast a ballot than there are those who stay to discuss and watch proceedings. Proponents of either viewpoint usually are not hidebound in their ideas, and many, including the writer, feel that a real study should be made of the status of local voting before saying definitely that either system should be used to the exclusion of the other.

Having said all this, it is necessary to insert one note of caution. The old Town Meeting is not possible where towns have hundreds or even thousands of voters. There is no structure in many of these towns large enough to accommodate all who might wish to come and the Australian ballot must be used. One answer to this situation is the representative town meeting now used in Brattleboro, where approximately a hundred and ten citizens are chosen to assemble in a Town Meeting, and to vote for and in the name of their eleven thousand fellow citizens.[18] Except for choosing representatives to this type of Town Meeting and deciding certain other questions, such as the sale of fermented beverages and liquors, where this system is used there is little need for the Australian ballot.

One further point in favor of a representative town meeting is that nominations for officers must be made and filed not more than twenty-eight days nor less than twenty-one days before the annual meeting.[19] This advance nomination prevents the questionable

---

18   No. 302 of the *Acts of 1959*, pp. 428 - 433   .
19   24   VSA   §   726.

deals and peculiar activities that have sometimes shadowed town meetings, and to that extent must be commended. The reverse of the coin is that even this action may not produce worthy candidates because of pressures exerted on citizens to run or not to run for reasons that have little to do with community welfare. Town government is not easy nor should it be whimsical, but the product of thoughtful considerations and judgments.

CHAPTER 25

Town Representation in the
General Assembly

All the laws and regulations pertaining to towns which have been discussed above have been the work of the General Assembly of Vermont. Under the Constitution this body is given the task of enacting the laws which are to govern the citizens of the state. Because of this close tie with the people, the composition and representative nature of the General Assembly are important to every town.

The General Assembly now has two branches, the Senate and the House of Representatives, but this was not always the case. From 1778, until 1836, the General Assembly of Vermont was unicameral in form, and had only a House of Representatives.[1] In addition there was a Governor's Council of twelve men, elected to sit with the Governor and other officers as an executive council,[2] and a body of thirteen known as the Council of Censors.[3] The former, in some respects, served as a second chamber and to the extent it did so, weakened the idea of a single-chambered legislature. The latter body was to be elected at seven year intervals, beginning in 1785. The functions of the Council of Censors were to see if there had been any infractions of the Constitution; to see if there were laws that should be repealed; and to propose revisions of the Constitution. Although these two bodies could exert pressure on the General Assembly, the Assembly was almost independent and did its work alone.

The *first* constitution provided that the Representatives were

---

1 *Constitution of 1777*, Chapter II, Sections I & VIII.
2 *Ibid.*, Chapter II, Section XVII.
3 *Ibid.*, Chapter II, Section XLIV.

164

to be chosen annually in September by the qualified voters in each town. No person was eligible for the office until he had lived in the state and in his town for one year.[4] In order to provide for equitable representation, the constitution also provided that any town with eighty or more taxable inhabitants should have two representatives, and that all other towns should have one.[5] This was to be followed for seven years, and then representation was to be one from each town.

In addition to these stipulations, the founding fathers stated that representatives were to be persons who were "most noted for wisdom and virtue" in the towns of their residence.[6] In all the years that have elapsed since then, this requirement has never been waived or changed; these words should be noted carefully at every election. As has so often been the case, there should be no automatic election to the General Assembly merely because it is the "turn" of some citizen in the town to go to Montpelier. It needs also be pointed out that sometimes a very interesting interpretation has been given to "most noted for wisdom and virtue" when a town elected some character to go to Montpelier in order to relieve the town of his care for the period of the session, or to prevent his going on the town quite so soon.

The first constitution fixed the term of the representatives at one year. This was because of the colonial fear of persons in office; the fathers seemed to think that there was something baleful about an election that changed an otherwise good man into an evil agent looking for the destruction of his fellows. Fortunately, this earlier mistrust no longer has the paralyzing grip on popular imagination that it once had. But it was not until 1870 that the constitution was amended to give the representatives a two year term of office, with biennial sessions of the legislature. The two year term still holds.

The passing years have brought many changes in the manner of nominating and electing the Town Representative. The first provisions in the *Laws of 1779* stated that the qualified electors of the several towns were to meet on the prescribed day in September and

---

4 *Ibid.*, Chapter II, Section VII.
5 *Constitution of 1777*, Chapter II, Section XVI.
6 *Ibid.*, Chapter II, Section VII.

cast a ballot for the person of their choice. The ballot was to be folded and handed to the presiding constable, who upon the closing of the polls, would count the ballots and announce the results.[7] By 1797, the law provided that the voting for Town Representative was to be completed in the space of two hours, while balloting for the Governor was to proceed for a total of four hours.[8]

There is no need for an historical survey of the various changes in nomination and election procedures except to say that in 1915 the General Assembly first provided for primary elections to nominate the candidates for office. There are now two elections every even year — the primary on the second Tuesday of September to nominate the candidates of the several parties for all offices,[9] and the general election on the first Tuesday of November to elect the officers so nominated.[10] Of the two elections the primary is the more important. This was particularly so in the years from 1915 to 1961, when Republican nomination was tantamount to election. The old tradition of 109 years toppled when in 1962, Governor Hoff was elected as the Democratic Governor of Vermont.

A person who wishes to be a representative from his town must circulate a petition, and secure the names of legal voters of the town equal to three per cent of the total votes cast for all the candidates for representative in the last preceding election.[11] When the required number of signatures has been secured, the petition is to be filed with the town clerk not less than forty days before the primary election.[12] The names of all the persons who file petitions which bear a sufficient number of valid signatures, and whose petitions are otherwise in order, will be placed upon the primary ballot.[13] At least forty days before the primary the Secretary of State is required to inform all the town clerks in writing that the election will be held, and to furnish each clerk a list of the offices to be fill-

---

7   *Laws of 1779*, p. 37. (Incidentally, ballot boxes were not authorized until 1815. *Laws of 1815*, Chapter CXXXVII, p. 159.)

8   *Laws of Vermont*, 1797, Chapter LVII, p. 547.

9   17   VSA   §   301   to   §   517.

10   *Vermont Constitution*, Chapter II, Sections 35 and 36;   1 VSA § 117;   17 VSA § 1421.

11   17   VSA   §   336   (3).

12   17   VSA   §   340.

13   17   VSA   §   334, 337.

ed. The town clerk must post a notice in three public places in the town within a period of ten days after receiving the communication from the Secretary of State. These notices must include the time and place of holding the election.[14] The general statutory provisions call for the primary election to open at ten in the morning and close at six in the evening, at which time the ballot boxes are turned and the ballots are counted.[15] The person who receives a plurality of votes for representative in each of the parties is the candidate of that party, and will be voted upon in the general election.[16]

At the November election the candidate who gets the largest number of votes is declared elected, and will represent his town in the next session of the General Assembly.[17] In case of a tie vote for representative the presiding officer is to recess the election for one week, posting notices in three or more public places in the town, stating the day and time of such recessed election." At the new election the voters are to cast their second ballot, which includes the absentee voters balloting under new provisions.[18] If there is again a tie vote, it appears that a third ballot must be cast in accordance with 17 VSA § 1141, as it has been changed by No. 198 of the *Acts of 1963*.[19] These new statutes change practices that have been followed for decades.

The constitution still provides that each organized town have one representative to the General Assembly.[20] Today the lower house contains 246 members; one representative each from 238 towns and 8 cities, and constituencies range from 38, to over 35,000. There is always a question as to whether a body of this size can truly be a representative body, or whether it will be controlled by a small minority that knows exactly what it wants — there are just too many persons present to permit a full and free dis-

---

14   17   VSA   §   333.
15   17   VSA   §   381. This seems now to be superseded by 17 VSA § 1048 which was enacted in 1963, and sets different hours than the accustomed ones.
16   17   VSA   §   384.
17   17   VSA   §   1181, as amended by No. 231 of the *Acts of 1963*, pp 259 - 260, temporary edition.
18   *Ibid.*
19   17   VSA   §   1141.
20   See note 5 above and the text it verifies.

cussion of issues. Yet without this discussion the majority tend either to vote blindly, or on the mere say-so of their more politically sophisticated colleagues. Either method is open to criticism.

The first constitution attempted to provide equality of representation and succeeded to a high degree. However, inequities soon became apparent and in order to correct them the Council of Censors, when they met in 1785, proposed two new alternative methods of choosing the representatives to the House. It is worthwhile to quote in full these suggestions for a smaller and more representative House, as they were set forth in the proposed draft of the Constitution:

Sec. VII. To prevent unnecessary expense in legislation, for the more deliberate and expeditious proceeding in that important business, and that the freemen may be better and more equally represented, the whole number of Representatives in Assembly shall not exceed fifty; to be elected in manner following:* . . . each organized town in the State, on the first Tuesday in September annually, shall have liberty to choose one able, discreet freeholder, to represent them in a county convention, to to be held at such time and place as the Legislature shall by law, appoint; the members of which conventions, when met, shall, by ballot, elect from their own body so many of said representatives (to consist of persons most noted for wisdom and virtue) as the legislature shall, in future, limit, having respect to the grand list of each county, in apportioning the number.

* The Council of Censors, also propose, instead of the remainder of section VII, the following clause, to be at the election of the convention, viz: — the Legislature shall, in their first session after the approbation of this section of the Constitution, (having regard to the grand list, the local situation of, and the probability of a disproportionate increase of population in the different districts) divide the whole state into fifty districts, to continue for three years next after the division and provide for the due and orderly election of one representative in Assembly from each district, and in such manner that the votes shall be received in the respective towns. That the Legislature shall have power, if a different increase of population in the respective districts shall render it necessary twice in each septenary, forever hereafter, and no oftener,

to divide the said districts in a more equal manner.[21]

The Convention that met in Manchester in 1786, did not see fit to make use of these suggestions of the Council of Censors and the original *arrangement* remained in the *Constitution of 1786*. However, it is interesting to note that even at that early date some of the citizens were not satisfied with the inequalities that had appeared at that time. The census returns for 1791 show that the fears of inequality voiced in 1785 were not without foundation, for towns varied in population from a minimum of three in Hardwick and ten in Morristown, to 2,350 in Bennington, and 2,422 in Guilford.[22] The first two towns apparently sent no representative to the General Assembly for several years.

The latest census in 1960, shows some very interesting statistics that bear out the fears of the fathers in 1785. The ten smallest towns in Vermont had a total population of 661, while the ten largest towns had a total of 132,250, persons, or 200 times the population of the ten smallest towns. Yet each group of towns had ten representatives in the General Assembly. Twenty-five of the largest towns and cities in the state had a population of 204,863 or 52.5% of the state's total, yet they had only 10.16% of the vote in the lower House of the General Assembly. Also the 124 smallest towns that have a majority vote in the House have only 11.8% of the population.

Although the problem of inequality has been stated, this writer sets forth no solution, because any that might be offered, has in all probability been aired before. The legislative committees appointed in 1939, 1949, and 1959, to propose amendments to the Constitution all were presented with requests to change the inequality and all acted as if there was a loss of hearing involved. As matters now stand, the General Assembly almost exemplifies the position of "taxation without representation" that so aroused the American colonists prior to 1776. Since it is wholly possible for any session of the legislature to remedy the inequality without a constitutional amendment, it is hoped that the spirit of fair play will soon change

21   Slade, *op. cit.*, p. 520.

22   Edward Conant, *The Geography, History, Constitution, and Civil Government of Vermont*, 5th ed. revised and enlarged by Mason Stone, Rutland, 1907, pp. 95, 99, 103.

the situation where the votes of a tenth of the population of Vermont are only worth one nine hundred and ninety-fifth of the vote of the citizens in the smallest town.

SECTION V

Conservation Problems

CHAPTER 26

Land Abandonment

Town government in Vermont is essentially rural government, and as such depends for its support upon taxes levied on the basis of land values. It has already been shown how custom and the law place the chief tax burden upon real property. Consequently any major reduction in either the value of the land, or in productive use of the land, will have very adverse effects upon local government; this is the reason that the abandonment of cultivable lands in Vermont is a serious matter. A period of great loss of farmer population through migration from the land occurred in the last three decades of the 19th century. The same problem agitated the whole of New England; the lure of cheap, fertile, western lands drew many persons away from the homes of their fathers. Since the turn of the century the mass migration has slowed down, but there is a steady decline in the number of farms and in the population rate of growth.[1]

The peak number of farms in Vermont was reported in the federal census of 1880, when there were 34,522 listed. By 1900, the number had fallen to 32,890, and by 1940, to 23,582. But the demands of the war years and the reuse of formerly empty farm houses increased the number of farms until in 1945 they numbered 26,490; these census figures listed many more farms than were actually used by the owners to make a living from the land. For a time after World War II this classification may actually have increased as some returning veterans tried out their hands at farming,

---

1 The beginnings of this movement can be fully studied in Lewis D. Stillwell, *Migration from Vermont*, Montpelier, Vermont Historical Society, 1948.

173

just as their fathers did before them following 1918. However, in a few years the rate of farm abandonment again increased, because even with modern methods, many persons found that they could not scratch a living out of hill farms. So much was this true that by 1962, the census bureau reported only 12,099 farms in Vermont, and of this number probably half are either not farms at all, or at best, part-time farms. In 1962, the State commissioner of Agriculture reported that there were only one-third the dairy farms there had been twenty-five years before. Notwithstanding this loss, these farms were producing fifty per cent more milk on greatly reduced acreage.

This rapid abandonment of farms and the loss of population is cause for real alarm about the future of towns in Vermont. Every year several hundred more farms are closed. The local papers are full of notices of sales of farms and announcements of auctions of equipment as the land owners are no longer able to keep up with farm work because of age, the inability to hire help, or because their families have largely gone elsewhere in the hope of gaining a better living. In many cases these abandoned farms are sloping hill farms which probably should never have been operated at all. In a more primitive society where wants were few, horizons limited, and competition was slight, families could wrest a living from the slopes; but it cost the entire farmily, from small children up, endless hours of often fruitless labor. Today such lands are called sub-marginal and society understands that it has to pay heavy social costs to maintain families in such sterile areas. No amount of romanticizing by antiquarians can make conditions on such a place acceptable when status is measured by flush toilets and TV sets. There is no reason for weeping when such farms are abandoned for tillage and turned to a more effective use, such as a permanent program of tree planting; there are problems when the weary land is permitted to produce only scrub second-growth trees.

The major ill-effects from farm abandonment come when fertile valley farms are closed out. Because there is usually a road in the valley, one of the prevalent happenings today is for the land to be sold to "summer people" who are looking for a "place in the country." At first the new owners are too busy rebuilding and "restoring" their home to do much with their land, and it only takes a few years of neglect for scrub trees to appear and for useless brush to choke up the pastures. Constant effort is required to keep land productive for any useful purpose. Other losses in good valley farm lands have come from highway construction and flood control projects.

In every town an effort should be made to keep the best land in full use and at top production. To do this may require some concerted community effort, for at any given time there may be no one farmer who is able to make the payments required to procure and operate the land about to be abandoned, and there will be need for cooperative financial help. This is not to say that there should be no sale of land to those looking for a vacation home, or retirement retreat. Far from it. If there is no one living in a farm home as such, then by all means sell it to someone who will keep it habitable. The same might be said about developing the rocky-untillable knoll with a magnificent view. But very few such purchasers want to, or know how to run the complicated business which farming is today, and some would not have the necessary capital to restock the farm if they did. It would be better to sell only the farm home and a few acres around it; the rest of the land would still be available for farming or tillage, if it were valuable for this purpose. The new owner and the town should find it possible to get together on the usage of the land so that each would understand the other's point of view. The primary responsibility for initiating such a discussion rests with the selectmen and listers and the Planning Commission as discussed below.[1a]

It is not fair to new owners that that they be "soaked" to support others. This is often done by assessing the new residents for the full value of the former farm, even though the land is idle and non-productive. This is done because it is felt that the "sun-tanner" is fair game, otherwise he wouldn't have been so foolish as to buy the old place anyhow. Neither is it right to allow good land to lie fallow and cause the reduction in local property values. It is here that cooperation could save the land for proper use; the financial future of many towns depends upon solving this problem. Unless all rural livelihood is going to be based on services rendered to tourists, there is a real need to salvage agriculture by retaining the tillage of valley fields and the pasturage of gentle hillsides.

1a See Page 183 below.

CHAPTER 27

Population Decline

The steady loss of population in rural Vermont still goes on as farms close and the former owners retire to the cities or move to other states for more lucrative employment. The rate of population increase is the slowest of any state in New England, and almost in the nation of those states showing an increase. The growth in the few larger centers tends to hide the general losses everywhere else; this is no new phenomenon but is of old lineage. In 1911, Mr. William Rossiter presented a startling paper on the decline of population in Vermont that is still significant and the situation he described still continues.[2] One of the maps which illustrated his report showed all the towns in Vermont that had had a continuous decline in the census figures at every census from 1850 to 1910.[3] There were 46 of these towns — a fact which no one else had taken the trouble to point out. In the 1960 census nine of these same towns showed a decline in every census after 1910, or a steady decline for 110 years. One of the towns, Somerset, was disorganized by the legislature of 1937. The other thirty-six had had from one to four population increases since the 1910 census, but every one of the forty-five had fewer people in 1960 than they had had in 1850, and only five had more than in 1910. In the state as a whole 188 towns had fewer people in 1960 than they did in 1850, while 138 towns lost population from 1950 to 1960.

From the state as a whole, eight counties lost population in the

---

2 William Rossiter, *Vermont, An Historical and Statistical Study of the Progress of the State*, in American Statistical Association, New Series, No. 93, March 1911, pp. 388-449, and 5 maps.
3 *Ibid.*, p. 418, Map #9.

fifty years from 1910 to 1960, while Chittenden County during the same years gained over 31,000 of the total 33,000 increase. The tendency for most of the towns to lose population is of long standing, and the more rural the town the greater the proportionate loss. Every county reported at least one town with a population increase, and every city save Barre had a larger population in 1960 than in 1910. The towns surrounding all the cities except Vergennes show-ed appreciable effects from their proximity to the city. Where there was a substantial business enterprise that afforded an opportunity for employment the town showed a population improvement. Thus in those towns where population has grown the loss in agriculture has been cancelled out by industrial activity. But in those towns where new ski developments are taking place an increase in the tax base has not yet been accompanied by a corresponding increase in population.

While no conclusion can be reached from a small sampling, it is nevertheless interesting to speculate, and two towns are used here as illustrative of population trends. The town of Benson has decreased in every census since 1850, save 1950, when its population was one person larger than in 1940. The town of Marlboro decreased in every census from 1850 to 1940, and since then has increased its population because of the establishment and growth of a small college. These two towns show certain interesting features in the following data from 1910 to 1960:

MARLBORO

Population		Grand List	Tax Rate	Amt. Raised By Taxes	Per Capita Tax
1910	442	$2,203.16	$2.00	$ 4,406.32	$ 9.97
1940	225	$1,970.65	$3.75	$ 6,289.75	$27.95
1960	347	$5,943.26	$5.60	$33,282.26	$95.91

The tax rate increased 85% from 1910 to 1940
                                49%   1940   1960
                               280%   1910   1960

The taxes raised increased about 50% from 1910 to 1940, about 500% since 1940, and 800% since 1910.

The population has increased 54% since 1940, and still has 21.5% fewer persons than in 1910. The per capita costs increased 343% since 1940, and 962% since 1910.

BENSON

Population		Grand List	Tax Rate	Amt. Raised By Taxes	Per Capita Tax
1910	813	$4,767.29	$1.50	$ 7,150.94	$ 8.80
1940	572	$5,018.00	$3.40	$17,164.40	$29.66
1960	549	$7,129.09	$6.30	$44,875.48	$81.74

The tax rate increased about 127% from 1910 to 1940
                              85%   1940   1960
                              320%   1910   1960

The taxes raised increased about 140% from 1910 to 1940, about 161% since 1940, and 528% since 1910.

The population has decreased 4% since 1940 and 33% since 1910. The per capita costs have increased 275% since 1940, and 929% since 1910.

There is no way of measuring the actual cost relationship between these towns because we do not know the comparative assessment ratios, or the relative effectiveness of the services rendered. But, although it can be assumed that the efficiency of the two governments has increased because of the demands of the people, and that the costs are not as great as the figures show because of the cheapening of the dollar, it is still true that these small towns, along with many others, are bearing a greater burden of government costs than they can support. As long as the same or better services have to be supplied in all towns in spite of dwindling populations, the costs levied on those who remain are constantly to increase. This fact requires some thoughtful consideration of the future of these towns and this in turn raises questions about the sufficiency of the area in a town to support a government.

CHAPTER 28

Water Pollution

Every year the state's press and radio carry notices that the inhabitants of specified towns or villages will have to boil their drinking water before using it, and in every case, the causes are stated to be pollution of the water sources. Usually the circumstances are due to negligence, or apathy toward the shameful pouring of filth and offal into the water supplies. With reasonable precautions, the only times when such notices are called for are when some natural catastrophe like a major flood disrupts man-made installations.

Modern civilization is based upon large quantities of pure water to a degree that few people comprehend. Without pure water none of our cities could exist as they do today, and little of our food would be safe until everything was boiled or cooked. Life would be considerably less pleasant than it now is. Unfortunately, the amount of good water available for use is always limited, although many people feel during a prolonged wet spell that the supply is inexhaustable. The limited supplies are often strikingly illustrated, as was the case in Ohio during the war when certain critical plants were forced to slow down and restrict production because the ground water supplies upon which they depended were being used too rapidly. Another example which comes easily to mind is the annual drawing of water to which some Vermont dairy farmers are forced during a long dry spell.

Since the supply is limited, it is imperative that what there is should not be spoiled by pollution; the best way to prevent pollution is for each locality to handle its own problems, and before contamination becomes serious. The failure of Vermont towns to take this kind of action has meant that both the State and National Government have been forced to step in, and now the towns have little recourse save to carry out the instructions from above.

The town in Town Meeting assembled can take steps to see that individual homes in the town are required to dispose of their wastes in a harmless manner by installing septic tanks or some other safe disposal method. If there are already sewerage systems that have outfalls into streams or lakes there can be a vote to build a disposal plant to remove and prevent pollution. The necessity for care is well represented by the experience of Milton Village several years ago when the water test showed typhoid bacilli, and the water all had to be boiled. The water system was based on a carefully regulated water shed and it was only after long and careful search that the course of the trouble was found in the sanitary facility of a lumber camp built directly over a tiny stream flowing eventually into the reservoir. The popular belief that running water purifies itself did not prove valid here.

Fifteen years ago there were only two sewage disposal plants in operation in the state; today (1963) there are fourteen, with seven more under construction and others being considered. The towns now have full authority to build, equip, operate and maintain water systems, sewerage systems, and sewage disposal plants. They may even create separate corporations to place the costs upon the participants and not the area as a whole. In every instance the action is voluntary and requires a vote of the citizens to validate the procedures and expenditures.[4] In recent years Congress has provided federal funds, to be matched by state funds, which are available to the towns for planning and constructing sewage disposal plants. Each town desiring to make use of the money must vote a prescribed portion of the total cost before it can use the grants.[5]

In addition to the erection of plants, the towns can vote for the necessary regulations to prevent the dumping of industrial wastes into streams, be it from sawmills, manufacturing plants, creameries, or dyeworks. These industrial wastes are often just as harmful as human wastes. It is mostly apathy that prevents such steps from being taken, for the costs are soon repaid in better health and in pure water supplies. No one person or company should be permitted to continue the process of destroying one of nature's best gifts

---

4   10   VSA   Chapters 73, 75, 77, and 79.
5   24   VSA   §§   3614 - 3618.

to Vermont — her water supply.

There is a growing desire on the part of Vermonters that "Unspoiled Vermont" be true in fact, and there has been considerable legislation on the subject of water control. Ever since 1947, there has been a state board, now Vermont Water Resources Board, to regulate, or prevent, pollution of water.[6] It has been given extensive duties,[7] and is to act in conformity with the terms of the New England Water Pollution Control Compact.[8] Also, the law now prohibits the creation, increase, or change in pollution as it existed on June 1, 1949, unless the board mentioned above, grants the right to do so after a petition and investigation.[9] The prevention and reduction of water pollution goes along at a slow rate; the board and its employees have done a great deal of work but without full public support. As towns and persons fail to respond voluntarily it becomes more and more evident that coercive powers will soon have to be granted to the board to enforce its requests. This is true also of the work of the State Board of Health and its control of pollution.[10] Were each town or neighboring towns, in cases of necessity, to take the steps permitted, the state boards could devote their energies to more constructive efforts than trying to persuade people to refrain from present practices. There is no better way to kill off a thriving tourist business than to continue to pollute the waters of the state so that they will be unfit for domestic or recreational purposes.

---

6   10   VSA   §§   571 - 576.
7   10   VSA   Chapter 33, §§ 901 - 1053.
8   10   VSA   §§   991 - 1002.
9   10   VSA   §§   909, 910.
10   18   VSA   §§   1201 - 1217.

CHAPTER 29

Planning and Zoning

In preceding chapters there has been a discussion of several factors which tend to weaken local government by dissipating or destroying the natural resources which sustain an active economic community. The abandoned and rundown farms tend to drain away the support of government for useful services and place the support in areas where it is less effective: as fewer and fewer productive acres remain it is increasingly difficult for them to supply the funds for schools, for roads, and for public needs in general. Under these circumstances it is important for all towns to give attention to local planning and its complement, local zoning. To be successful, a combination of these two concepts is required. Planning is an overall program for determining the most advantageous use of land and buildings; zoning is the creation of specific laws to regulate this use by districts. Many persons attack planning because it means stock taking ahead of time, and to them any planning involves coercion. To others, planning and zoning are the panacea for all local government ills. The actuality lies somewhere between these two extremes.

To a discerning individual a minimum of investigation will show the need for planning and the consequences of not doing so. Unfortunately, it has been true that when an area or country is new and developing almost no one thinks of planning and zoning, and by the time the need is seen it is too late to correct most of the errors in land use which have by then been made. When conditions are primitive and the land is raw each new home is started when and where each pioneer desires, and some of these homes are located most advantageously. Other persons settle on land that is not capable of supporting them and their descendants, and the property eventually is abandoned after causing a great waste of human effort.

In Vermont the necessity for planning has been evident for many years — in fact, a hundred years ago voices were raised requesting that plans be made to prevent the great loss of population to the western states. A more recent plea for planning and zoning was found in an editorial in *The Newport Express*. Here the editor was proposing that the towns invest in cellar holes. By this the editorial writer meant that the towns should purchase run-down and out-of-the-way farms and tear down the houses. The land so purchased was to be made into a town forest, and money saved through not having to plow the winter roads and keep up the other civic enterprises in the area was to be spent on the more prosperous areas which already furnished the money. In this manner the editor hoped to improve the status of local government by concentrating expenditures where they would do the most good.

Planning can be used to correct and to prevent a disregard for economic realities. The collective intelligence of the community is tapped for the information which can forewarn those who try to live in unsuitable surroundings, or under impossible conditions. Any town can now vote to create a five member Planning Commission[11] which has broad powers to create a comprehensive plan for future development, and also to propose the main outlines of a zoning ordinance.[12] A plan, once accepted by the voters, becomes binding upon all within the town and no public buildings, roads, or public enterprises can be constructed until the proposals for such have been submitted to the commission and accepted within thirty days.[13] Control of subdivisions can be given to the commission, and when this is done all plans must be submitted to the body, which holds public hearings on the matter and decides to approve or disapprove within a period of forty-five days.[14] The subdivider may be required to post a performance bond for the proper construction of the streets and improvements on them. The bond may run for three years and failure to carry out the improvements may lead to forfei-

---

11   24   VSA   §   2901.
12   24   VSA   §   2904.
13   *Ibid.*, Sec. 3.
14   24   VSA   §§   2905 - 2909.

ture and the carrying out of the work by the municipality with the funds received.[15] By March 1, 1963, twenty-six towns and cities and one village in Vermont had individual planning commissions. Some have been very active; others started out well but lack of local support has stalled further proceedings; some have merely been authorized.

Since 1957, the law has permitted two or more towns to create a joint or regional planning board, which, when set up by mutual consent, has all the powers and authority within the region that the town planning board has in the town.[16] In all cases the law specifically authorizes the town or towns to pay the expenses incurred by the commission, thus truly validating the whole procedure. Unfortunately little formal regional planning seems to be in effect in 1963, but Barre City and Barre Town are engaged in joint planning and have employed experts to do the task. In Caledonia, Essex, and Orleans Counties (The Northeast Kingdom) a great deal of organized work at public expense for the development of the region has been done, but so far no binding regional regulations have been adopted.

The conduct of the zoning process presupposes long range planning of a purposeful and permanent nature and requires legislative permission. The General Assembly granted this permission and since 1931[17] a clear statement permits towns to create and accept zoning ordinances. The law provides for rural and urban zoning, but basically both must follow the same rules.[18] When the citizens of a town, by a vote at a properly warned Town Meeting, have given the authority to the selectmen to provide for town zoning the selectmen then appoint a zoning commission. This commission is to study the town, propose the division into districts in which the different regulations are to apply, issue a preliminary report, and schedule a public hearing. The sense of the hearing is to be incorporated into a final report which the commission makes to the selectmen.[19] The selectmen then draw up a proposed zoning ordin-

---

15 24 VSA §§ 2910 - 2912.
16 24 VSA §§ 2919 - 2922.
17 24 VSA §§ 3017 - 3021.
18 24 VSA §§ 3022 - 3026.
19 24 VSA §   3013.

ance which the law states shall try ". . . to lessen congestion in the streets; to secure safety from fire, panic and other dangers; to promote health and general welfare; to provide adequate light and air; to prevent overcrowding of land; to avoid undue concentration of population; to facilitate the adequate provision of transportation, water, sewerage, schools, parks and other public requirements . . ." This broad grant of power is given in order to provide for ". . . conserving the value of property and encouraging the most appropriate use of land throughout such municipality."[20] The ordinance is to apply in the districts proposed by the zoning commissioners and provided by the selectmen, and each district may have its own rules.[21]

The selectmen are to hold a hearing on the proposed ordinance, giving at least fifteen day's notice of the session.[22] If no change is required the selectmen then call for a vote on the proposed ordinance, giving at least thirty days notice and circulating the proposal by posting in each polling place in the town and printing the document in full in some newspaper of general circulation in the town.[23] A favorable vote authorizes the enforcement of the ordinance. No existing usage of a non-injurious nature can be prohibited by the ordinance;[24] but future development of non-conforming use or additions to existing structures may be.[25] Provision is also made for the creation by the selectmen of a board of adjustment to hear and adjudge complaints or mitigate hardships by open hearings properly publicized.[25] These actions are taken following an appeal by the injured party, and careful statements are made in the law to protect all persons interested. There is little chance for wrongful practices.[27] Finally, the way is left open for appeals to the county court where the matter can be thoroughly reviewed.[28] On paper these procedures appear to take but a short time, but in actual practice they may

---

20 24 VSA §   3009.
21 24 VSA §   3005.
22 24 VSA §   3011.
23 24 VSA §   3003.
24 24 VSA §   3010.
25 24 VSA §   3020 (2), (13).
26 24 VSA §§ 3014 - 3016.
27 24 VSA §§ 3017 - 3021.
28 24 VSA §§ 3022 - 3026.

stretch out over a period of several years before an acceptable ordinance is adopted.

The same techniques are used with respect to homes and buildings within prescribed districts as are applicable to land. It is poor policy to permit construction of homes that are not up to certain standards of safety, or shanties and shacks which soon become a drain upon town finances. The zoning can be accompanied by the appointment of building inspectors[29] and wiring inspectors.[30] Joint work by these officials would help prevent many of the fires which now impoverish the country-side. Proper inspection at stated intervals would mean a close check on electrical wiring and equipment so that hazards could be eliminated before disaster struck. The saving of even one good farm home and its outbuildings would more than justify the cost of inspections for a long time.

The planning commission has a great responsibility for it is really determining how the town is to grow and develop; zoning in a town affords an opportunity to protect the general welfare. Wherever it has been tried, most people are unwilling to return to old practices, and the towns are better able to handle their own problems. This makes them less dependent on outside help, or less subject to outside orders. Zoning is town activity at a very high level. This is rapidly being understood and in early 1963 there were sixty-four towns in Vermont with zoning programs in effect or studies going on. Thirty towns were operating under self-drawn and accepted programs.

In connection with zoning, brief mention should be made of the pioneer program in Wisconsin. Early in the Depression local government was in such desperate straits that the legislature was forced to act. Counties were granted the right to vote on the adoption of zoning laws which cut across town boundaries. If there was a favorable vote the county was divided into three classes — first, a forestry area devoted to tree culture in which no one could live; second, forestry and recreational area in which people could live only during the summer or vacation period; third, the area designated farmland where people lived the year round. It was only in class three area that schools, roads, and other public services were

---

29 24 VSA §§ 3101 - 3117.
30 24 VSA §   1033.

permitted. Access roads only were found in class two. Many counties in northern Wisconsin gratefully accepted these arrangements and soon found that there was an improved standard of living for everyone. Families were encouraged to move from the first two class areas and resettle on class three lands where they were better able to make a living; towns no longer had to support families on worn-out or useless soils by paying them to live there as was done whenever the family income was based on local road work, payments for transporting their own children to school, or on welfare grants. Such families usually had paid no taxes and were a net drain on the community. The towns then bought up vacated lands and farms and added them to the forest system or recreational area. Both parties gained. The resettled farmer had good land and *paid* taxes, the town had woodlands that would eventually bring revenue to the town. The principle of zoning had rehabilitated families and had helped save local government.

CHAPTER 30

Town Forests

According to law a town, as a municipal corporation, is supposed to be perpetual, that is, it will go on forever. Since this is the expected life of a town, any given set of citizens or town officers has a definite responsibility not only for the present but for the future. Too often in the past this fact has been disregarded, and today many towns suffer in consequence. Nowhere is this seen more clearly than in the forest lands within a town's boundaries; they have been exploited and soil exposed to erosion with never a thought of the morrow.

Although the terrain in Vermont is rugged and the granite of its hills lies near the surface, the state is fortunate in the fact that it is in a belt where trees naturally grow well. Originally most of the more than 9,000 square miles of the state were covered with fine stands of timber — some trees being more than eight feet in diameter; all early accounts of the state seem to stress the abundance of this great resource. Today only small tracts of virgin timber remain, and these exist because it has been too difficult to log them off. The climate and other conditions which made the great forest possible still remain and quality trees could be caused to grow once again. There is no reason why large areas of the state should not be returned to timber production and the mature trees used as a basis for a perpetual income.

But when large areas of forest lands have been as completely cut-over as they have been so often in Vermont, it takes many years to bring them back into a state of production. Practically no persons and few companies are able to tie up their capital for a half-century or more, as is necessary for effective reforestation, and Vermont's

archaic forest land tax system discourages individual property owners from far-sighted forest husbandry. Any individual may be able
to set aside a few acres of land in forest for his grandchildren but the
gesture is of little overall value when there are millions of acres
which need attention.

A way out of this dilemma is for the town to take over the
vacant and unused land, plant trees, and manage the new forest
as a business proposition; the town can afford to take over some
of the land and to wait decades for its profits, and in the meantime
its holdings are increasing in value with each passing year. It is
not necessary for the towns to take over all the available land
within their boundaries for there are some companies and corporations which will be ready, willing, and able to undertake some long-
range forest projects. Before long under any system the annual
growth will require a periodic thinning process which will bring in
sufficient income to pay for supervision and maintenance, and with
proper management the sale of marketable timber from the town
forests will be regularized and be expected to furnish a good part
of the town's income in perpetuity.

Led by public spirited citizens and town officers, 104 towns,
cities, and villages in Vermont had municipal forests in 1962 with a
total of over 37,000 acres. Another 12 towns had forests of less
than the 40 acres required to classify them as town forests. Since
1951, every town and village is required to add an article to the
warning for Town Meeting asking for a vote on the establishment
of a town forest.[31] The article must be inserted until there has been
an affirmative vote, after which the town is deemed to have com-
plied with the law.[32]

Legal authority for the expenditure of town funds for securing
land for town forests was first provided by the General Assembly in
1915. The legislation provided that any municipality might "at any
legal meeting grant and vote such sums of money as they may deem
best for the purchase, management, and improvement of lands
for the purpose of growing wood and timber thereon."[33] It also
provided that if the property so owned totaled at least 40 acres the

---

31   No. 74 of the *Acts of 1951*, 24 VSA § 2407.
32   24   VSA   §   2408.
33   No. 24 of the *Acts of 1915*, pp. 84 - 85.

state forester would make a free examination of the area and give his advice as to what trees should be planted. The forest was to be a school endowment forest,[34] but this was changed to a municipal forest in the revision of the laws in 1917.[35]

There have been a few changes and amendments in the first law. The state will now pay half the cost of securing land for a municipal forest up to a total of $600 for each town during a biennium. If that much is not needed for the land, the remaining state money can be used to pay for trees and their planting. The state forester is to supervise the cutting of the trees in these forests, and to act in an advisory capacity.[36] If the town sells the forest the state money must be repaid to the state.[37] The purpose of the law seems to be to help smaller or poorer towns get started in the establishment of a municipal forest.

Although a town may vote on acquiring a town forest at any Town Meeting the requirement for the vote is often a futile gesture unless explanations and preparation have been made ahead of time. Many years ago the state forester outlined certain actions which would be valuable in gaining public support.

1. Create a committee to study the proposition and make a formal report to the Town Meeting.
2. Get local Service Clubs and other organizations to back the town forest.
3. Have a group or several groups raise money to buy land and present it to the town.
4. Use the town watershed as a town forest.
5. Use the Town Farm as a town forest. [This proposal was made when there were such farms. As they were abandoned for welfare purposes many were actually used in this manner and this explains the size of some forests.]
6. Make the town forest a memorial to the men of the town who have served their country in time of war. [This suggestion seems much better than erecting a stone or metal monument.]
7. Get many individuals to buy and donate one or more acres of land in the proposed forest as a gift to the

---

34 No. 24 of the *Acts of 1915*, pp. 84 - 85.
35 No. 254 § 477, of the *Acts of 1917*.
36 10 VSA § 1673.
37 10 VSA § 1674.

town.[38]

No matter what procedure is followed, once a town forest is created the town has a source of revenue, its waste lands are revived, there can be a good watershed, and recreational programs can be proposed.

Two municipal forests in Vermont are often cited as outstandining examples of successful programs. Rutland city has the largest municipal forest in the state with 4700 acres of trees covering its watershed and helping to preserve its soil. During the Depression the forest furnished cordwood for relief purposes and now through selective cutting furnishes both lumber and cordwood with a return over the past four years of $23,677, or an average of $1.25 per acre.[39] Eventually the return may be much larger. The officials in Rutland who purchased the land in 1910 at a cost of about $60,000 were not shortsighted; the city still has the land and a productive forest and the Rutland water supply has been an additional bonus. Competent authorities have estimated that a town forest of 2,000 acres will have a value of $100,000 after thirty years and an annual income of $4,000 to $20,000.

Essex Junction Village seems to have the oldest town forest in Vermont; the officials began to acquire land for the purpose in 1890, and today it covers 800 acres. The cost of the land and the planting and care of more than a half million trees since 1910 has been met by the sale of cordwood and lumber. Other forests might be discussed, but it would repetitious of the above. Each forest is managed under the supervision of the state forester and the plan is for selective cutting of mature trees so there will be a continuous supply of logs. Those who know about these programs need no urging to continue their expansion; those who do not know about them need only to be shown.

Municipal forests are not new. The town of Newington, New Hampshire, has had a town forest since 1710. Although it is only 110 acres in extent, it has played an important role in the life of the town, supplying timber for its meeting house, schools, church,

---

38 *Forestry in Vermont,* Department of Forests and Parks, 1947, p. 23.

39 *Biennial Report of the Department of Forests and Parks, 1961 - 1962,* p. 20.

and other public buildings and serving as a park for the townspeople. Lately it has supplied beams for town bridges. European states have had municipal forests for centuries. Anyone who has seen the carefully tended and productive forests of Switzerland, France, or Germany will understand how valuable they are. It has been estimated that in normal times these forests return $10 to $12 per acre of trees as income to the municipalities, and in addition furnish work for many citizens of the cities or villages, and a supply of wood and lumber for the industries and occupations that depend upon this raw material.

An example of community planning could be well emulated in Vermont. A town in Arkansas purchased its own forests and trees with the expectation of economic survival based upon these holdings. Instead of using thirty per cent of each cut tree as is customary, the town's wood processing plants have been attempting to use seventy per cent or more, and the material that is left over at the end of processing is used as a ground cover and mulch under the growing trees. Waste has been greatly reduced.

By covering its watershed with trees, a town (or several towns) will guarantee its water supply. At one time the streams of Vermont flowed clear and had a remarkably stable volume, a matter of comment by all observant early visitors to the state. It is doubtful if there were the spring floods that now cause so much trouble. The area was covered with forests and under the trees there was a heavy forest mulch that was able to absorb, hold and slowly release fifty per cent of its volume in water. As the forests have disappeared so has the forest litter and the streams are now seasonal — so much so that personal and municipal water supplies are often undependable. Vermont depends upon surface water for most of its consumption, and the loss of the forests means that there are no longer the reserves which once kept the streams flowing.

CHAPTER 31

The Green Mountain National Forest

In connection with public forests in Vermont mention must be made of the Green Mountain National Forest which lies along the ranges of the Green Mountains from Addison County to the Massachusetts border. It is composed of two large areas of land containing about 580,000 acres, of which 232,134 acres have been purchased from private owners by the National Government. It took special action by the General Assembly to make these purchases possible and the state has reserved certain rights, even though the land has been sold to the national government.[40] The Forest is run on a multiple use basis, with lumbering, soil conservation, recreational, and hunting and fishing aspects all given their place.

The Department of Forests and Parks reports that thirty-three towns have land in the Forest and in 1962, the cash payment to these towns amounted to $69,623.53.[41] This sum represented twenty-five per cent of the gross revenues of the Forest and is paid to the towns in lieu of taxes on the lands taken; the payments amounted to nearly thirty cents per acre and represent the same sum as if the town had levied a stumpage tax of twenty-five per cent. In addition the towns have certain of their roads and bridges in the Forest maintained by the Forest Service. The land is properly maintained by selective cutting of mature trees; there is no clean cutting of the vegetation leaving the land unproductive for years. Ten to twelve million board feet of lumber are taken annually from the Green Mountain National Forest and the figure is expected to rise to fifteen million or more board feet as the trees mature.

---

40 No. 3 of *Acts of 1935*, 10 VSA §§ 1605 - 1609.
41 *Biennial Report, op. cit.*, p. 49.

The state forester estimates that in Vermont, forests could grow on about 4,000,000 acres of land. This comprises areas now in forest, in useless brush, or in abandoned farm lands that are reverting to trees and is two thirds of the area of the state. The Green Mountain National Forest boundaries enclose some 580,000 acres and the national government hopes to own about 485,000 acres eventually. The prices paid for this land have been higher than the average for other national forests but the Forest is more productive than almost any others in the East. When the total proposed national forest acreage is subtracted from the state acreage that will grow forests, there are still 3,500,000 acres left. Since town forests cover only 37,269 acres there is plenty of area left for every town and city to acquire sizeable tracts without harm to even the most reluctant owners.

Almost every town in Vermont is constantly on the lookout for some type of industry that can add to the economic stability of its people. Even in their depleted state the forests of Vermont furnish employment for 7,000 to 10,000 workers in sawmills and industries dependent on wood and wood products, not to mention farmers and other workers who supply the raw materials. There is a steady decline in wood-working establishments and two reports dated 1947, and 1962, clearly show it. The comparative figures show 535 sawmills in 1947, and 297 in operation in 1962, with 80 idle plants; there were 182 woodworking industries in 1947, and only 61 in 1962, with an additional 12 not operating. In view of an overall consumption of wood and wood products greater than growth replacement, it would seem that nearby forests should be able to provide townspeople with added industries. This is particularly true since research constantly discovers ways to use woody material that was formerly considered waste.

CHAPTER 32

The Towns and New Industry

Almost every Vermont town is on the lookout for some type of industry that can add to the economic stability of the community Most persons know that it is risky for a town to depend entirely upon one industry or occupation, for there are bound to be periods when any one product is not in demand. A new plant comes into being when the raw materials with which it works are available in a location that is satisfactory in relation to a market. It also requires a labor force that is adequate in numbers and capable of performing the necessary tasks. Most of Vermont has long fulfilled the requirement for market and labor force, and has been weakest in raw material supply; it is in this connection that the perpetual resource of well-managed forests on the hills and mountains of Vermont assumes such significance. The labor force in the state has been such that skilled work was possible and it was profitable to bring in and manipulate high cost materials of small bulk. Today as automation and electronics demand new standards, it is questionable whether the schools of Vermont are turning out nearly enough qualified workers for this newer type industry.

A study of the official directory of manufacturing establishments in Vermont discloses that there are more products made and handled in the state than the ordinary person realizes. This has been borne out by the two industrial displays at the University of Vermont in recent years. Also, a quick tour around the state leaves a visitor amazed at the number of small-to-medium plants that help to swell the incomes of thousands of persons. In many cases these workers own small farms or acreages upon which they raise a substantial portion of their food. A combination of industrial work and subsistence farming has long been held by many authorities to be the most satisfactory kind of livelihood; it makes for security and stability, and this in turn gives useful citizens to the community. The shorter work week now in prospect makes this combination even more possible than formerly, and the availability of small acreages is one of the state's assets.

But even though an effort is made to bring in new industries, each town must be careful to find plants that are either stable, or give promise of being so when fully developed. There is a tendency to try to inveigle industry into a town by making concessions and promises. State law provides that tax exemptions can be granted industries by a vote of the town[42] for a period not exceeding ten years. This is, for the most part, a risky procedure. Any company that is so shaky that it is tempted to come because of the exemption from local taxes is probably going to be a poor asset to the town, and probably will not pay adequate wages in the bargain; ordinarily local taxes make up but a small per cent of the costs of operation. Many communities in this country have made tax concessions lasting for a number of years only to find that the day the concession expired the company folded up and moved on; a company that has once been bribed will be likely to move when the next bigger bribe is offered. The only justification for a tax concession is when a company has to spend some years in installing and testing very expensive equipment, and each year sees real value added to the non-operating plant. In such a case the town could well afford to exempt the property until production began, and perhaps at the most, for one year of production. With such an outlay a plant is not going to move, and in the installation period tax concession has merit.

It is equally questionable to give a company property which has been purchased with tax money. To prevent some of the difficulties which arise when towns give property to industry, the General Assembly in 1955, gave permission for towns to borrow the money to build a plant and to amortize the bonds, issued to pay for the project, over a period of years by renting the property to interested companies.[43] The certificates of indebtedness are not liens on the town and are not to be taxed by any local or state agency.

---

42   24   VSA   §   2741,   32   VSA   §   3834.
43   No. 255, of the *Acts of 1955*,   24   VSA   §§   2701 - 2714.

The law has been used several times and seems to be a happy solution to the problem — a company has a ready built plant, the community has a new industry, and a business transaction of value to all has been consumated.

Any new industry will cost the town money for additional government services — there will have to be more police protection, more fire protection, more sewers, more and better water, good schools, and good roads. A really good business will consider these factors far more valuable than a temporary tax exemption, and will be willing to pay its share for these services.

SECTION VI

The County and Its Problems

CHAPTER 33

County Organization

Even though the town is the basic unit of local government in Vermont, this state, like all others, has found it necessary to have a level of government between the town, or other local governments, and the state government. The county has been assigned this position from the first days of the country's history, for it came to the New World with the first English immigrants. Counties have been known in England for centuries, and before they came into existence as such there were the earlier shires. Almost from the first days of the Massachusetts Bay Colony settlement, the General Court found it necessary to group several towns together as a county, largely to provide a base for judicial support and activity, and from that day to the present this has been the role assigned to the counties of New England.

Because of a different set of economic conditions, the colonies south of the Mason-Dixon line created counties which became the chief unit of local government in that area. The large plantations and the slave economy prevented the development of villages, and this in turn made town government almost impossible, so that it never put in an appearance. The patterns thus fixed in the early days continued until the two streams met in the Middle West in the 19th Century. There the county form of government won out, largely because of the greater distances and the much larger farm holdings than had been the pattern in New England. County government in the South and West is thus very different from that in New England in general, and in Vermont in particular.

There are fourteen counties in Vermont in 1963. In 1778, there were only two. Then by successive acts of the General Assembly the state was further sub-divided until by 1797, there were eleven counties, which covered the state.[1] In 1802, Grand Isle County was carved out of portions of Chittenden and Franklin counties.[2] In 1810, Jefferson County was incorporated,[3] only to have its name changed to Washington County in 1814,[4] and in 1835, Lamoille County was chartered.[5] The number thus established has remained unchanged, but there have been many minor changes and revisions in their boundaries.

These fourteen counties have, in general, only two functions to perform: to serve as the base for judicial process, and to act as an election unit.[6] In the latter capacity the counties are used for the election of Senators to the General Assembly. But even here, the ballots are cast and counted in the towns, and the returns sent to the county clerk for canvassing. He then certifies as to the total votes from the county for each candidate, and notifies the successful ones of their election.[7]

It is the judicial aspects of the county that are most important. Each county has a county court held in the shire town at least twice a year, with certain specified exceptions.[8] There are six Superior Judges who preside in these county courts in a specified circuit from county to county and which is arranged by the body of Judges.[10] The judges are ranked in seniority according to their first election by the General Assembly.[11] The term of office is two years but the superior judges are usually relected for as long as they wish to serve. Biennially, each county elects two Assistant Judges who sit with the Superior Judge in the County Court. Two judges constitute a quorum,[12] but in case any of the judges is disqualified to sit on a case. the others, or even one judge, may preside over the court and

---

1 *Laws of Vermont*, 1797, Chapter VI, pp. 129 - 133.
2 *Laws of 1802*, Chapter 84, p. 141 - 143.
3 *Laws of 1810*, Chapter 74, pp. 101 - 103.
4 *Laws of 1814*, Chapter LXXIX, pp. 83 - 84.
5 *Laws of 1835*, No. 41, pp. 30 - 31.
6 See *supra*, p. 5.
7 *Constitution*, Chapter II, Sec. 37.
8 4 VSA § 115.
9 4 VSA § 71.
10 4 VSA § 73.
11 4 VSA § 71.
12 4 VSA § 111.

hear the case.[13] There is also at least one Municipal Court in all of the counties whose jurisdiction, with three exceptions, extends throughout the county,[14] and there are one or more Probate Judges in every county.[15] These latter courts probate wills and handle matters pertaining to estates. They perform one of the vital functions of government and consequently are carefully regulated by law.

There are other county officers connected with the enforcement of law, but they are not jurists. Each county has a Sheriff.[16] This is an old and honorable office going back to the early history of England. For many years the shire reeve (who later became the sheriff) was the chief official in the English county. The duties of the office gradually changed and have changed over the years in this country until today, in law, the sheriff is an officer of the court and chief law-enforcement officer of the county.[17] He is also the keeper of the county jail.[18] Practically, however, the sheriff's law enforcement duties have been assumed by the State Police forces, leaving the sheriff to the tasks of court officer and server of legal documents for a fee. The sheriff appoints deputy sheriffs in each town or city, and they serve in his stead in cases of a local nature.[19] They also serve as the nucleus for a powerful political machine for the sheriff. In every county a High Bailiff is elected whose sole duty is to arrest the sheriff if or when necessary, and to perform the sheriff's duties under these circumstances.[20] The last official here is the State's Attorney, who is elected to prosecute cases in the name of the State before the Court and to fulfill other required tasks.[21]

Finally, there are several other county officers who have limited functions to perform. There is a County Clerk, appointed by the Assistant Judges for an indefinite term,[22] who acts as a clerk of the

---

13   4   VSA   §   112.
14   4   VSA   §   421, as amended in 1959.
15   4   VSA   §§   271 - 277.
16   *Constitution*, Chapter II, Sections 35, 45.
17   24   VSA   §§   291 - 309.
18   24   VSA   §   297.
19   24   VSA   §§   307 - 309.
20   24   VSA   §§   331 - 332.
21   24   VSA   §§   361 - 364.
22   24   VAS   §§   171.

County Court and performs for the county the same functions which the town clerk does for the town. There is a County Treasurer,[23] a County Auditor,[24] and a board called Commissioners of Jail Delivery.[25] In spite of the fact that the county has limited functions, the tasks of these officials are detailed and often important in their own right. Without counties there would be greater burdens imposed upon town and state officials, with probably lessened effectiveness. The counties also serve as clearing houses and repositories for many legal documents, and can provide the duplicate copies of many of them. In these ways the counties in Vermont do serve the people of the state, but are less vital than are the towns.

---

23 24 VSA §§ 211 - 224.
24 24 VSA §§ 261, 262.
25 24 VSA §§ 401 - 404.

CHAPTER 34

County Representation In The Senate

Although each town has its own representation in the House of Representatives of the General Assembly, a different pattern is used for the Senate. Here the county is the unit for the election of Senators. The background for this variation is found in the early history of the state. When the first Constitution of Vermont was drawn up at Windsor in 1777, the Convention provided for a single House of Representatives and placed the supreme legislative power in its hands[1]. Provision was also made for an Executive Council of twelve members,[2] plus the Governor and Lieutenant Governor.[3] This body was given the power to scrutinize, and either give consent to, or hold up legislation, but this suspensive veto held only for a period ending with the next meeting of the General Assembly.[4] The Executive Council was also given authority to assist in choosing the Governor, in case no candidate should receive a majority of the votes cast by the electorate for the office.[5]

Since the powers granted to the Executive Council were not truly legislative, it meant that Vermont had a unicameral or one chambered legislature. Both Pennsylvania and Georgia also had unicameral legislative bodies, but by 1791, each had adopted a two chambered structure. Vermont retained the single chamber un-

---

1 *Constitution of Vermont,* 1777, Chapter II, Section II.
2 *Ibid.,* Chapter II, Section III.
3 *Ibid.,* Chapter II, Section XVII.
4 *Ibid.,* Chapter II, Section XV.
5 *Ibid.*

til the Convention of 1836,[6] when it adopted the proposals of the 1834 session of the Council of Censors which had called for the creation of a Senate. Similar proposals had been made by the Council of Censors at seven year intervals, starting in 1792, but the conventions representing the towns had turned down the proposals. The late Daniel B. Carroll told the story of the refusal to create a second chamber in his study, *The Unicameral Legislature of Vermont.*[7] In 1835, because there were three parties in the field, no candidate for governor recevied a majority of the votes of the electorate, and the choice was thrown to the House of Representatives and the Executive Council. Inter-party strife precluded compromise and no governor was elected for the term and the Lieutenant-Governor had to take over. Coupled with some high-handed refusals to accept the vetoing of House bills, this disgraceful episode aroused the public to protest against the House, and caused the election of delegates to the Convention who were willing to abolish the Executive Council and create a Senate as an antidote to the House.

It is worth noting that the decision on the retention or abolition of the Executive Council and the creation of a bicameral legislature was not made on its merits, but was made because of extraneous political factors that had little to do with the matters in hand. Many of the proponents of the bicameral system advanced arguments for that system similar to the arguments used today by those who advocate a return to the single-chambered legislature. It was argued that there would be greater efficiency if there were two chambers, that legislative costs would be less, and that better laws would result. Professor Carroll showed how none of these factors carried much weight in the actual decision, and that the reasoning

---

6 This Convention, and the preceding seven such gatherings beginning in 1786, was the body called into being by the Council of Censors to accept or reject that Council's proposals of amendment or censure. The Council of Censors provided for the membership and election of the Convention, which usually consisted of one representative from each town, and was regularly outstanding in its lack of comprehension of the changing times and its refusal to accept the progressive amendments proposed by the small, thirteen member Council of Censors.

7 Carroll, Daniel B., *The Unicameral Legislature of Vermont*, Montpelier, The Vermont Historical Society, 1933.

that finally carried the day was that Vermont should not be different from other states! If Vermont wanted to conform to the general pattern, there would have to be a bicameral legislature. On this note Vermont created the Senate.

The new Senate was to have thirty members chosen from the freemen of the counties of the state — a requirement still present today. Each county was to have at least one senator, and the rest of the body was to be apportioned to the counties on the basis of their population as ascertained by the last census, giving attention to the county with the greatest fraction remaining over the figure set for representation.[8] The number of senators from the different counties has varied with the changing population of the state. In 1951, and during every other session in the 1950's as well, the legislature refused to reapportion as called for by the Constitution, and again in 1961, took no action. A special session in the summer of 1962, passed a temporary act to expire December 31, 1963, which gave Chittenden County one additional senator at the expense of Rutland County. Since this was a temporary act of expediency only, the basic questions of representation with regard to the population of the counties and of the validity of the legislators' oath of office still remained unanswered. (The 1963 legislature extended the life of the act until December 31, 1965. This was in anticipation of a court decision which might change the ideas of the legislators.) Because the population trend in Vermont is for the larger places to increase and those with small populations to shrink, the quibbling and delay merely mean that rather than regular shifts at a slower pace greater shifts will have to be made at one time. The Senate now has five persons from Chittenden County; three each from Rutland, Washington and Windsor; two each from Addison, Bennington, Caledonia, Franklin, Orleans, and Windham; while the four remaining counties have one senator each.

Each of the Senators must be a freeman of the state, a resident of the county from which he is chosen, and at least thirty years of age.[9] Members of the House need be but twenty-one.[10] Although the age requirement is higher, the senators usually are no older on

---

8   *Constitution*, Chapter II, Section 18.
9   *Constitution*, Chapter II, Section 18.
10   *Constitution*, Chapter II, Sections 13, 15.

the average than the members of the House, and there are those who claim the senators are younger. Both Houses are equal in status except that revenue bills must originate in the House. As a general rule the senators seem to represent their counties and satisfy their constituents.

CHAPTER 35

The Assistant Judges

In the United States the county has sometimes been called the most useless level of government, a judgment which seems to be more valid in New England than in the western states. But wherever one may be, the county violates a basic shibboleth of American doctrine, since in the county there is no separation of powers, nor are there three branches of government. This is true to an extreme degree in Vermont, where the only elected officers are those concerned with law enforcement, and yet to some officers are also assigned certain non-judicial and administrative functions. It is necessary, therefore, to discuss the position of assistant judge in its administrative aspects. The technical legal and judicial duties of the assistant judges are not taken up here, for such a discussion is not a function of this document.

The *Constitution of Vermont of 1793,* provided that the General Assembly was to "elect" the judges of the county and superior courts.[1] This included the Assistant Judges and remained the law until 1850. In that year the constitution was amended to permit the freemen of each county to elect two assistant judges who were to sit with the superior judge in the county court. Today these two judges are elected to office on a party ticket, the same as any other officials. Each aspirant for the position must file a petition containing the names of a least two per cent of the number of persons who voted for the office in the last election. The properly signed petition is filed with the county clerk,[2] who verifies the signatures and, if they are adequate, is required to place the name of the candidate

---

1 *Constitution of 1793*, Chapter II, Section 9.
2 17 VSA § 336.

upon the proper ballot prior to the September primary election. The two candidates from each party who receive the greatest number of votes are listed on the county ballot for the general election in November.[3]

It is probably in order to digress a moment to explain how political figures are placed in judicial posts in this way. From the 1770's, the freemen of Vermont have felt the necessity of electing all officials, including judges. In the early days any man whose judgment was respected could be elected a judge by the legislature, and the early court records show a very high proportion of lay judges. As the notion of using trained lawyers as judges grew, the freemen held even more tightly to the concept of assistant judges who, it was felt, knew the local conditions and consequently could temper justice with mercy. Although of equal status on the bench with the presiding judge, they seldom exercised their prerogatives, leaving the legal matters in the hands of the lawyer-judge. The aura of the past still clings to the position, and even today, once elected assistant judge, the title is retained for the few remaining years of the life of the official. (Nearly all the assistant judges are retired men who crave something to do.)

It is quite remarkable that these elderly men can carry out the numerous administrative tasks imposed upon them — but they do. First of all, they are charged with the care and upkeep of county property.[4] They are responsible for buying as much land as may be required for county purposes — the decision in this case being left to their discretion.[5] The assistant judges are charged with the upkeep of the courthouse in each shire town; they must provide and maintain offices for the several county officials, and vaults and safes for storing records and files;[6] they must furnish telephones to the several county offices,[7] and a portion of the janitor services. The state of Vermont pays for the heat, lights,[8] and such portion of the janitor service as the state finance director deems equitable.[9]

---

3   17   VSA   §§   383 - 384.
4   24   VSA   §   131.
5   24   VSA   §   77.
6   24   VSA   §   71.
7   24   VSA   §   75.
8   24   VSA   §   74.
9   24   VSA   §   72.

They are responsible for procuring and maintaining jails, and certain county law enforcement equipment.[10]

The mere listing of these functions gives but an indication of the trouble and difficulty that is sometimes involved in their execution. The assistant judges get the money for these costs of operation by ordering the county treasurer to issue warrants to the town treasurers calling for the collection of the county tax,[11] and to the state finance director for unorganized towns and gores within the county.[12] The amount of the tax will have been decided by the assistant judges, who will have fixed a figure which will pay off any county indebtedness due, as well as the current costs of operation. The law places one obstacle in the conduct of this county business; the total tax levied may not exceed five cents on the total grand list of the county. Prior to 1957, the limit was two cents.[13]

The assistant judges are also required to appoint certain county officers. Most of these appointments are for a two year term, beginning February first of each odd year, and holding until a successor is appointed and qualified. First in importance among the appointed officers is the County Clerk. He is the one official who has an indefinite term, holding his position at the pleasure of the assistant judges.[14] The salaries of the several county clerks are fixed and paid by the state and range from $1000 to $5750 per year.[15] There is a County Treasurer appointed for a two-year tearm.[16] Like the county clerk, he must be bonded in a manner satisfactory to the assistant judges,[17] and receives a salary fixed by them. He is required to handle the county funds and to make an annual settlement with the county auditor, then turn the statement over to the assistant judges,[18] who are required to publish it.[19]. The assistant

---

10   24   VSA   §   75.
11   24   VSA   §   133.
12   32   VSA   §   4965.
13   No. 3 of the *Acts of 1957*, p. 4.
14   24   VSA   §   171.
15   32   VSA   §   1181.
16   24   VSA   §   211.
17   24   VSA   §   212.
18   24   VSA   §   221.
19   24   VSA   §   224.

judges also appoint the County Auditor for a two-year term.[20]

The assistant judges themselves, together with the county clerk, serve as a Board of Jury Commissioners.[21] The judges appoint three Commissioners of Jail Delivery every two years,[22] whose duty it is to investigate the situation of a debtor lodged in jail, upon his request, and, if he is able to take the poor debtor's oath, release him from jail.[23] The assistant judges also appoint as many Notaries Public in the county as the "public good requires."[24] Certain other related tasks are given to them in addition to their technical legal duties when the county court sits, and consequently, it is easily seen that there is more to the office than might be supposed. For all their work, the two men receive ten dollars per day for the time they are in court, or are actually performing their official responsibilities. They may also receive their necessary expenses, but the total received makes the office more of an honorary one than one sought for its pay.

---

20 24 VSA §§ 261, 262.
21 12 VSA §   1403.
22 24 VSA §   401.
23 12 VSA §§ 3671 - 3693.
24 24 VSA §   441.
25 32 VSA §   1141.

CHAPTER 36

The County Clerk and Other Officers

After the assistant judges, the most important county official is the County Clerk. Since he is appointed by the judges for an indefinite period, it is customary for this official to serve in his post for many years — a change ordinarily occurs only when old age forces out the incumbent. Most of the duties of the county clerk are those known as ministerial; that means that the tasks of the office are carefully prescribed by law, and the clerk has little opportunity to exercise discretion or to act in this way or that. While a goodly portion of his work is thus quite routine with the same tasks recurring periodically, it is still true that unless he does them well the county and its inhabitants suffer.

By virtue of his appointment, the county clerk is also clerk of the county court and must keep the records of all the proceedings therein.[1] He prepares the docket for the court and the attending attorneys.[2] He, or the sheriff, is to open and adjourn the court from day to day, if there are no judges present on the prescribed day.[3] It is his duty to act as an *ex officio* member of the Board of Jury Commissioners. This is the body which makes up the list from which grand and petit jurymen are drawn each year. The county clerk receives a list of names from every town clerk in the county, equal to ten per cent of the legal voters in the town, but in no case is the town list to contain more than a maximum of fifty names.[4] When it has been properly drawn, the clerk has the custody of the

---

1   4   VSA   §§   601 - 602.
2   4   VSA   §   603.
3   4   VSA   §   151.
4   12   VSA   §   1403.

final list and is an active participant when the names of the jurymen are drawn from this list for active duty in a session of the court.[5]
It is the clerk's responsibility to ask the State Finance Director for
funds with which to pay the fees of the jurymen who have served,[6]
and of witnesses as well.[7] He is required to issue the warrants for
payment and to keep track of the time served by each of the above
groups.

The county clerk must record all the documents, deeds, and
materials pertaining to the unorganized towns and gores within
the county.[8] He is also required to record any legal instruments
presented to him which pertain to property located in the county.[9]
This is often done by property owners to make sure that in case a
fire destroys the records in the town clerk's office, there will be another record of the transactions stated in the deeds. For these services the clerk receives recording fees which are prescribed by law.[10]

As an election official the county clerk is charged with the duty
of preparing, distributing, and paying for the ballots and sample
ballots used in the election of county officers.[11] He also receives
and records the returns for these same county officers so that a
final figure may be officially given.[12] He records the election of each
justice of the peace,[13] and certifies as to the fees and other payments
to them. When a justice of the peace dies, or resigns, his records
must be given to the county clerk for safe keeping.[14] Because the
clerk handles state and county money, he is required to furnish a
bond to the assistant judges under the usual legal stipulations.[15]
The clerk alone may appoint a deputy clerk for whom he is responsible, but the assistant judges fix the salary and provide for its

---

5   12   VSA   §§   1404 - 1405.
6   32   VSA   §   472. The rules for when fees are due are found
in 12 VSA, App. II, R. 52; and the amount of the fees to be allowed is
fixed in 32 VSA §§ 1511 - 1512.
7   32   VSA   §§   1551 - 1553.
8   27   VSA   §   403.
9   27   VSA   §§   401 - 402.
10   32   VSA   §§   1751, 1760.
11   17   VSA   §§   791, 806.
12   17   VSA   §§   1633 - 1636.
13   4   VSA   §§   491, 493.
14   4   VSA   §§   494, 496.
15   24   VSA   §   175.

payment.[16] For these and the multitude of other tasks connected with their work the county clerks receive stated salaries ranging from $1000 to $5750.[17]

The last two non-judicial officers of the county are the Treasurer and Auditor. The former has the greater amount of work to do, but even here, the burdens of office are not onerous. The treasurer must keep the financial records of the county and has the custody of county funds, and is bonded like any other financial officer. He is required to care for the glebe lands and land granted for the care and support of ministers and churches, so far as they lie within the boundaries of the unorganizeed towns and gores in the county. He collects the rent due from anyone using county property, and makes an annual report to the assistant judges, who then publish it.[18] The county auditor performs the usual functions inherent in such a title. He is also charged with the duty of turning over the books, papers, and county property in the custody of a retiring treasurer to a new one, when a change is made.[19]

---

16 24 VSA §   176.
17 32 VSA §   1181.
18 24 VSA §§   211 - 224.
19 24 VSA §§   261 - 262.

CHAPTER 37

Justice Of The Peace

In the several states each unit of government is rather closely linked with all the others, be they large units or small. This inter-relationship is clearly seen in the Justices of the Peace, who are called town officers and are elected by the towns, but who are county judicial officers whose responsibility is the enforcement of state laws. In Vermont, as in all other states, the justices of the peace are the lowest in rank of all that body of officers known as magistrates. Many people live their entire lives without having seen any other judge in action, and often the concept which the public holds concerning "justice" in general is derived from its experiences with, or knowledge about the justices of the peace. It is important, therefore, to discuss this omni-present officer of the law.

The American justice of the peace comes from the office of the same name in England; it has a history that is known to extend back at least to the 12th Century, and it may have been present even earlier in form, if not in name. For the three hundred years prior to the middle of the last century the justice of the peace was perhaps the most important local official in England. Beginning as an officer who had to have noble rank, the incumbents developed into a class of capable administrators. These representatives of the local nobility learned how to get along with ordinary citizens and how to conduct themselves in adverse and contentious situations. As they developed in skills they gained in powers, until at last they were practically, in themselves, the local government of England. They controlled the services for the poor, they enforced the law, they tried criminal cases, and were responsible for keeping the King's peace. It is not surprising that the position came to be one of honor and importance, and was much sought after by the gentry.

215

For many years the justices of the peace were unpaid, and they were untrained when they assumed office — only with experience could they become learned in the duties of the post. The government of England found it necessary to have some of these magistrates trained in the law, and those so trained were given a stipend for their services. Eventually the laws required that there be at least one of the *Quorum,* or paid stipendaries, in each panel of justices who were to try certain types of cases.

As early as 1630, the laws of Massachusetts provided for justices of the peace and they have been found in this country ever since. The use of untrained, and at the same time, responsible persons to enforce laws and to fulfill certain duties of government was almost a necessity in pioneer society. American history and folklore are full of tales in which a local justice had the affection of the community, as well as its wholesome respect. The first Vermont *Constitution of 1777* made the justice of the peace one of the county officials and provided that the time and place of his election be fixed by the General Assembly.[1] In addition, the members of the Supreme Executive Council[2] were to be *ex officio* justices of the peace with jurisdiction throughout the state.[3] They retained this right until the amendments of 1836 abolished the Council, and created the Senate in its place.

For some reason or another, the democratic method of electing the justices of the peace was abolished and, as set forth in the *Constitution of 1786,* they were to be elected annually by the General Assembly,[4] a practice which remained unchanged until 1850. The rules of that body prescribed that the delegation from each county was to hold a caucus and nominate the justices from their county who were to be elected by the General Assembly — the list thus drawn up and presented was ordinarily voted on without further comment. The old records show that from one to seven or more justices were elected in any given town. The constitutional amendments of 1850 restored to the people the right to elect the justices of the peace in their town.

---

1 Chapter II, Sction XXVII.
2 See above, pages 205 ff.
3 *Constitution of 1777,* Chapter II, Section XVII.
4 *Constitution of 1786,* Chapter II, Section VIII.

Justices of the peace have been elected biennially at the general elections in the fall of even years ever since the constitutional amendments of 1870. Five justices are to be chosen in a town with less than one thousand inhabitants, while a maximum of fifteen is elected in town with over five thousand population.[5] Before the newly elected justices of the peace may assume their office they must take an oath to perform their duties faithfully.[6] They are also sent a commission by the Secretary of Civil and Military Affairs in the name of and by the authority of the Governor.[7]

The first act prescribing the duties of a justice of the peace was enacted by the General Assembly in 1779,[8] and contained restrictions which have been present ever since. In England the justices of the peace were usually limited to criminal cases, but in the United States they were given jurisdiction in civil cases as well. In early Vermont the upper limit of value in civil cases was fixed at twenty pounds, and in criminal cases the fine could not exceed ten pounds, or the punishment of ten lashes of the whip. No land titles could be questioned in a justice court. These and similar restrictions were re-enacted in 1780, and 1782, and have continued to the present.

Since the justices of the peace are the lowest ranking magistrates in the hierarchy of judicial officials, in most minor cases their courts are the first to be used. In larger cities the justice courts have been superceded by the municipal courts,[9] whose jurisdiction is more extensive than that of the justices of the peace. The laws have taken away most of the criminal jurisdiction of the justices, and when they have anything at all to do, it is usually concerned with civil cases. Here in Vermont they are strictly limited to matters which involve less than $200. They may not preside in cases involving land titles, slander, replevin for more than $20 in valuation, and trespass where more than $20 is involved,[10] all of which means they handle very minor cases indeed. In any criminal case there is a similar restriction on fines and penalties,[11] but the law does permit

---

5   *Constitution*, Chapter II, Section 47.
6   *Ibid.*, Chapter II, Section 52.
7   *Ibid.*, Chapter II, Section 49.
8   *Laws of 1779*, p. 2.
9   See pp. 223 - 226 below.
10   4   VSA   §   503.
11   4   VSA   §   505.

the justices to handle more important matters in certain specified types of cases, and in these rare instances the justices may give a penalty more severe and a heavy fine. In all proceedings before a justice, the law prescribes a series of fixed fees which may be charged, and which constitute his recompense as the judge.[12]

Procedures in a justice court are less formal than in the county, or higher courts, but the justice has the right and duty to preserve order. The constable is the official who serves papers for the justice and who is to enforce order in the court.[13] The justice of the peace may issue warrants and other legal instruments that can be served by sheriffs and their deputies, as well as by the constable. In other words, the justice of the peace has the same rights and prerogatives on a small scale that judges of superior courts have on a larger and more important level.

In both civil and criminal cases, with certain listed exceptions,[14] the person who has received a penalty may appeal to higher courts, if he takes the appeal within two hours after the rendering of the decision.[15] This is a wise provision because so few of the justices have had legal training and their decisions might easily be wrong, or too severe. The chief exceptions to the lack of training are found in the larger cities and towns where some justices are chosen from among the lawyers in order to have the legal aspects of the office properly handled.

The justices of the peace may perform marriage ceremonies,[16] and they are required to turn the records of such action over to the town clerk who issued the license.[17] They are also to check for proof of the legality of the marriage, as is required of all persons empowered to perform the ceremony.[18]

The justices of the peace also have certain administrative functions to perform, just as their English precursors had. The most important of these is to serve with the selectmen and the town

---

12	32	VSA	§§	1756 - 1757.
13	4	VSA	§	507.
14	12	VSA	§	2623.
15	12	VSA	§§	2621 - 2622.
16	18	VSA	§	5144.
17	18	VSA	§	5146.
18	18	VSA	§	5145.

clerk as members of the Board of Civil Authority.[19] This board is the one that counts ballots at Town Meeting,[20] that gives its consent to prospective voters taking the Freeman's Oath,[21] and gives its advice on matters of similar import. The justices may also be called to serve on the Board for the Abatement of Taxes, which must by law, be called in each town every year.[22]

Currently, the laws governing the duties of the justice of the peace are scattered throughout the statutes and must be dug out laboriously—in this situation the justices of the peace and the selectmen are on a par. However, a further listing of the duties of the office would be an elaboration of related functions where, in some cases, the justice is required to take action himself, and in others, he can act only on the complaint of an injured party. Enough has been said to show the potential importance of an office that is often neglected, and is but partially understood by the townspeople. Vermont has hundreds of justices who hold a commission from the governor and do not know what to do with it or the office they hold. Some authorities say that efforts should be made to improve the qualifications of the justices by setting a minimum legal training without which no person could serve; other authorities say that it would be better to eliminate the office entirely as outmoded.

---

19   17   VSA   §   1.
20   24   VSA   §§   720, 731.
21   17   VSA   §   68.
22   24   VSA   §   1533.

CHAPTER 38

The Probate Judge and His Court

In every state in the Union there is an ascending structure of courts. In Vermont the lowest level is the justice of the peace court and the second is the probate court which stands next in line and below the superior court. The probate courts are on the general level of the municipal courts, but are considered of slightly less importance. This rating is strange, for they are responsible for some of the most important aspects of modern society. The laws of Vermont devote an amazingly large amount of space to a detailed description of the work and functions of the probate judge and his work.

There are nineteen probate courts in Vermont,[1] the General Assembly having united two of the oldest in 1957.[2] The general jurisdiction of the probate court is prescribed as follows: "The probate court shall have jurisdiction of the probate of wills, the settlement of estates, the appointment of guardians, and of the powers, duties and rights of guardians and wards."[3] These duties have come down through the years; the first laws passed in 1779, made provision for the settlement of estates and the probating of wills. While not as long and detailed as at present, the restrictions and regulations were fully as long in proportion to the laws of that date as they are today.[4] The material was largely borrowed from the laws of Connecticut, as they then existed.

Following provisions of the first constitution,[5] probate judges

---

1   4 VSA §§ 271 - 277.
2   No. 261, of the *Acts of 1957*, pp. 254-256.
3   4 VSA § 311.
4   *Laws of 1779*, pp. 39 - 40, 52 - 58, 78 - 79.
5   *Constitution, 1777*, Chap. II, Sec. XXVII.

220

are elected by the voters in each of the nineteen districts of the state.[6] In 1786, the General Assembly was given the right to elect the probate judge,[7] but the constitutional amendments of 1850 restored the right of election to the people. Since the constitutional amendments of 1870, the term of office has been two years. The term begins on February first after the November election in even numbered years.[8] When the election has been certified by the County Clerk, the Governor grants the commission to the newly elected judge,[9] which is his authority to perform the duties of his office.

So far as can be discovered there never have been any qualifications for the office except that the candidate must be the people's choice. With the detailed work and its volume, together with the necessity for accuracy and legality, this lack of qualifications is strange. By practice it has become quite customary to choose a lawyer for the position, and once elected, it is also customary to keep him in office about as long as he cares to serve. Thus, in practice, the people do what should be done by law. While there is no reason to think that the custom will be changed, better judgment would say that the time has come to set up real qualifications for the candidates for judge of the probate court.

The General Assembly creates the boundaries of the probate districts. Seven districts were established in 1779,[10] and had been increased to seventeen in 1797,[11] while by 1836, the twenty which covered the state until 1959 were well established. During the intervening years there were minor changes in area, but the names and meeting places of the courts were fixed. Most of the early requests for more and smaller probate districts have disappeared with the years; it is to be hoped that the pattern set in 1957 by the combination of the Addison and New Haven districts into the Addison district will be followed elsewhere. The proposal to have but one probate district in a county was made in the Report of the Commission on State Government and Finance which had been authorized by the General Assembly of 1945. The report brought about

---

6 *Constitution*, Chap. II, Secs. 35, 36.
7 *Constitution*, 1786, Chap. II, Sec. 9.
8 *Constitution*, Chap. I, Sec. 48.
9 *Constitution*, Chap. II, Sec. 49.
10 *Laws of 1779*, pp. 39 - 40.
11 *Laws of Vermont, 1797*, Chap. XVI, pp. 207 - 209.

a great political hassle but little came of it except the above mentioned action in 1957. No really valid arguments can be brought against this consolidation, except that it will remove a few political offices from the state total!

Each probate judge now receives a salary which is fixed by the General Assembly, and which ranges from $2,750 to $10,000 per year.[12] Formerly the judges also received the fees collected by their office, but out of their total income they were responsible for payment for their clerical assistance. The Commission, mentioned above, had pointed out that the fees received averaged from $556 to $8,590 per year above the official salary, with the result that salaries were raised and fees no longer added to them. This change has meant that some of the probate judges, as minor judges, no longer receive an income higher than any other elected official in the state, and in consequence, has reduced some of the complaints directed against the office. The fees prescribed for the services of the probate judge are set by the General Assembly and are very moderate in amount;[13] this principle of modest fees has been followed since 1779, and is to be commended.

In the past the probate judge appointed one or more registers of probate as needed, and for whose actions he was liable. He fixed their compensation and paid them out of his fees. Since 1957, the judge has appointed the registers but their salary is fixed by the state personnel director and state personnel board.[14] The same is true of extra clerical help and gives such appointees what amounts to permanence of tenure. Slowly the probate judge is becoming a professional, but it is only a question of time until the final acts are passed to make it a legal fact.

---

12   No. 278 of the *Acts of 1961*, p. 421.
13   32   VSA   §§   1433 - 1434.
14   No. 300 of the *Acts of 1957*, p. 326.

CHAPTER 39

The Municipal Court

In the United States we believe in a government of laws and not a government of men controlled by their whims; if there are to be laws there must be agencies to enforce them, and hence the court structure. It is now necessary to take up the two courts which play a major role in county government — the first of the two is the Municipal Court. Although they have been used for a long time, the name is of recent origin.

The first city charter of Vergennes, voted by the General Assembly in 1788, established a city court, which was to meet on the second Tuesday of every month.[1] The mayor and the first two aldermen elected at the annual meeting were to be the judges of this court; they were to hear cases involving citizens of the city, or a citizen of the city and a person from outside the city boundaries. No cases involving land titles were to be brought before the court, but in all other cases arising within the city, the city court had the same judisdiction that the county court had in the county.

As other cities and villages were incorporated by special acts of the General Assembly, provision was made for a police, city, or other court to have jurisdiction over criminal and civil cases, similar to those triable before justices of the peace. These special courts were to be presided over by men elected by the community and in some cases the judges were granted a small salary which was paid by the state. In 1890, the General Assembly decreed that the governor was to appoint and commission all the judges of city and municipal courts who were to receive all or part of their compensa-

---

1 *Laws of 1788*, p. 13.

tion from the state.[2] The new law was not to interfere with incumbent judges during the remainder of their term of office, but all future judges, appointed after November 1890 were to come under the act. The term of office was fixed at two years, instead of the previous one year term.

Today the statutes provide for seventeen municipal courts in the state.[3] The governor appoints and commissions the judges for a two year term, beginning February first of each odd year.[4] The judges must be freemen, and resident within the boundaries of the territorial jurisdiction of the court as established by the General Assembly,[5] except for the judge in Grand Isle County, who is to be the same judge as in Franklin County.[6] The judge has the right to make temporary appointments to fill his office in case of illness or absence; if he fails to do this an assistant judge is required to do so.[7] While there has been a custom for other judicial positions to remain in the hands of the incumbent as long as they desire to serve and are able to do their work, the municipal judges have become political appointments, used by the governor as a method of awarding faithful supporters. While in theory this should mean a lowering of the standards of judicial integrity, in this state this does not seem to have been the case. The position retains prestige, and because of the nature and amount of work performed, has in most instances been filled by qualified persons after careful, although political, consideration.

Municipal judges receive an annual salary ranging from $1,400 in Essex County to $4,050 in Chittenden and Rutland Counties. They also receive fees of $1.50 for each case recorded in the court, and fifty cents for each conviction report.[8] Since the judges are not in court all the time, ordinarily they may maintain their own legal practice, a matter of some moment in the fact of the low salaries. There has long been agitation to make the job a full-time one with

---

2 No. 73, of the *Acts of 1890*, pp. 74 - 75.
3 4 VSA § 421.
4 4 VSA § 432.
5 *Ibid.*
6 No. 142 of the *Acts of 1957*, Sec. 2, p. 125.
7 4 VSA § 433.
8 32 VSA § 1146, as amended by No. 241 of the *Acts of 1961*, p. 324.

an adequate salary, and the time may come when this will be an actuality.

The judge is to appoint a clerk, and may remove him at his discretion. Today, when once appointed, this clerk is a state employee and the salary is fixed by the state personnel director and personnel board according to the work of the office.[9] In the absence of the judge the clerk may act to continue a case, or to fix bail.[10] He is governed, paid, and acts under the same laws as a reporter of the county court; his accounts are paid by the state. The municipal court may hold sessions in the county courthouse, or in any other suitable quarters which may be found, subject to the consent of the state purchasing agent. The state pays for the care and upkeep of the courtroom.[12]

In the counties where there are municipal courts they have largely superseded the justice courts. The municipal court is given the same powers and jurisdiction as the justice of the peace court, and such other powers as may be granted specifically by the General Assembly;[13] its jurisdiction extends throughout the county in which it is located, with certain exceptions prescribed when there are two municipal courts in the same county.[14] The court is considered to be open at all times, and usually sits every day when needed except Sunday. Considerable discretion in these matters is left to the judge.

Procedure before the court follows that of the county court. Jury trials may be used, or may be waived by the parties to the case. The judge must keep a list of potential jurymen from which names may be drawn for jury service. The list must include names from every town in the county, with a total of not more than fifty persons from each town,[15] and is furnished in the same manner as the one for the county court. A sheriff or a deputy sheriff may be court officer, as may a constable, or any "indifferent person" when there is need.[16] These officers serve papers and make returns upon

---

9	4	VSA	§	641.
10	4	VSA	§	642.
11	4	VSA	§	740.
12	32	VSA	§	1147.
13	4	VSA	§	429.
14	4	VSA	§	421.
15	12	VSA	§§	1401, 1501.
16	4	VSA	§	434.

them in the usual manner.

A perusal of the daily press shows that the municipal courts are always busy. While cases are limited as to the amount of money or the severity of the sentence that may be imposed,[17] they make up in numbers what they may lack in importance. After a preliminary hearing in the municipal court,[18] cases involving serious crimes and larger amounts of money are transferred to the county courts.[19] In a few types of cases both courts have concurrent jurisdiction. Since minor infractions of the law are the most numerous, most people are limited in their knowledge to the courts of this level. When the caliber of work performed in the municipal court is high, the fair treatment accorded sets the tone for all law enforcement in the state.

---

17   4   VSA   §   422.
18   4   VSA   §   425.
19   4   VSA   §   424.

CHAPTER 40

County Courts

The last and by far the most important of the judicial agencies of the county is the County Court. The county court is presided over by a superior judge and the two assistant judges who have been discussed above. When the *Constitution of 1777,* was formulated at Windsor, it provided that "Courts of Justice shall be established in every county in this state."[1] Later in the same document the powers and jurisdiction of the Supreme and Superior courts of the state were set forth.[2] Still another section provided for the election of inferior judges by the people,[3] as has been outlined in earlier sections of this study. Finally, it was stated that the Governor and the Executive Council were to appoint and commission all other officers that were not elected by the people or by the General Assembly.[4] All these statements still left the election of the Superior Judges in an unresolved state. In the October 1779, session of the General Assembly, the omission was remedied by an act which said that because no particular method had been provided in the Constitution, ". . . in future the Judges of the Superior Court shall be chosen in October, annually, by the Governor, Council and House of Representatives, by their joint ballot."[5] Election by the General Assembly is still followed, but it is now biennially in the spring of the odd years.[6]

---

1 Chapter II, Section IV.
2 *Ibid.,* Chapter II, Sections XXI, XXII, XXIII.
3 *Ibid.,* Chapter II, Section XXVII.
4 *Ibid.,* Chapter II, Sections XVIII, XIX.
5 Slade, *op. cit.,* p. 391.
6 *Constitution,* Chapter II, Sections 42, 43.

In the beginning the same judges served on both the supreme and the superior courts of the state, and held terms of both in circuit around the state. The number of judges varied from time to time as the legislature changed its mind. At first there were five,[7] then three.[8] In 1849, the law was changed and provision was made for three supreme court judges and four circuit judges.[9] In 1857, the Circuit Courts were abolished and the number of justices increased to six.[10] In 1870, the number rose to seven;[11] in 1906, it fell to four;[12] and in 1908, it was again increased to five where it now remains.[13] In the 1906 general revision of the laws, the old concept of one set of judges was abolished, and two distinct series were established. Six superior judges and five supreme court justices were to be elected by the General Assembly biennially,[14] and this has been the practice ever since.[15]

During the years when annual election, either by the General Assembly and the Governor and Council, or later by the General Assembly alone, was the practice, there were frequent changes in the individuals elected as judges. The same name would appear for two or three years in succession and then not reappear for several years, or not at all. As the complexity of society increased and the need for trained judges became more apparent, there was an increasing tendency to re-elect the same men year after year. This tradition finally became fixed, and now when a man is elected for the first tims as a superior judge he is entering a life-time job, if he wishes it. He is regularly re-elected every two years, and eventually, through resignation or death of other judges who are his seniors in service, he is in line for election as a justice of the supreme court of Vermont. For practical purposes the two types of judges are but two divisions on separate levels of the same panel of judges. A judge

---

7   *Laws of 1779*, pp. 11 - 12.
8   *Laws of Vermont, 1797*, Chapter III, p. 76.
9   No. 40, of the *Acts of 1849*, p. 48.
10 No. 1, of the *Acts of 1857*, p. 4.
11 No. 1, of the *Acts of 1870*, p. 10.
12 No. 68 of the *Acts of 1906*, p. 68.
13 No. 57 of the *Acts of 1908*, p. 59.
14 No. 68 § 8 of the *Acts of 1906*, p. 69.
15   4 VSA §   71.

may serve in either capacity in case of need.[16] The superior judge, senior in terms of first election to his post, is considered the presiding judge and speaks for the group.[17] The six superior judges decide on their respective circuits of the counties of the state, and each serves in rotation in a separate section of the state.[18] The superior or county courts sit in each county at specified times and places in the fall and spring, [19] and in case of need a special term may be called for by the presiding judge.[20]

Although from the very beginning these judges have been chosen by the legislative body, the people of the several counties have been given the right to participate to some extent by voting for the assistant judges, as discussed above.[21] The two men sit with the presiding superior judge behind the bench, and it takes at least two judges to constitute a quorum for the transaction of business. If the docket is too crowded and a supreme court justice is called in to sit in a second court, one of the assistant judges must sit with him.[22]

No person is now elected to the position of superior judge until he has been scrutinized and recommended by the organized bar. This means that all of the endorsed candidates, usually members of the House of Representatives, are considered qualified, even though there is no guarantee that the winner will be the *best* qualified. By following the practice of adhering to the advice of the bar, Vermont has adopted an excellent method of choosing competent judges. By removing the position from the hurly-burly of political campaigns and providing for almost automatic re-election as long as competent work is done, the state is able to attract some of its best legal minds to the bench. This is demonstrated by the state's enviable court record.

The jurisdiction of the county courts is clearly set forth in the statutes.

---

16   4   VSA   §§   4, 74, 111.
17   4   VSA   §   71.
18   4   VSA   §   73.
19   4   VSA   §   115.
20   4   VSA   §   111.
21   See pages 208 - 211 above.
22   4   VSA   §   111.

Each county court within the several counties shall have original and exclusive jurisdiction of all original civil actions, except those made cognizable by a justice or municipal court, and of such petitions as may by law be brought before such court, and appellate jurisdiction of causes, civil and criminal, appealable to such court, and may render judgment thereon according to law.[23]

Further,

Each county court shall have original jurisdiction of of prosecutions for criminal offenses within their respective counties, except those made cognizable by a justice of the peace, and may impose sentence according to law.[24]

These terms mean that there are no top limits in civil suits, and that cases involving the death penalty as a maximum punishment are grist to the court. Decisions of the county court may be appealed to the state supreme court, which is the highest court in the state, but for all practical purposes because of the number and importance of its cases, the county court is the court of broadest scope. Although the Supreme Court has the final word in any case, it hears only a few each year and is thought of as the court of last resort.

The formal procedures before the county court, the method of trying cases, and the details of each official's work in the court are matters concerning the judicial branch of the state government as it enforces the laws, and are not properly the subject of discussion here. It is sufficient to say that all local officials and all citizens may be investigated, convicted, or exonerated by and before the county court; it is thus a method of control of officials in the name of all the people. In the eyes of the law *all* men are equally subject to penalties for wrongdoing. It is only thus that the self-government of a democracy is possible, and it is in support of this principle that Vermonters have stood on common ground.

---

23   4   VSA   §   113.
24   4   VSA   §   114.

Conclusion

When the towns of Vermont were first chartered, and began to function as units of government, they filled the needs of the times very adequately. Averaging about 36 square miles in area, they were in line with the transportation and communication facilities of the times, and they embraced about as much area as the comparatively scattered population could conveniently govern. Then the poor communications and the sparce population kept persons apart and prevented easy contacts; now the new gadgets make it possible for anyone to look in on his neighbor's dooryard at will. This change in living conditions has been paralleled by a steady increase in the costs of government; government and private activities alike are more costly and demanding than they once were. Each service has become more necessary and more expensive, and the taxpayers have had to bear the growing burdens which have resulted. Today many towns have too small a population to support satisfactory government services. To answer the demands of their citizens they have been forced to ask for help from the state, and indirectly, national governments.

Not only in Vermont, but also in other states, this necessity for help has grown steadily, and in return for aid with its promise of greater financial security, the local units have surrendered much of their freedom of action. The higher units of government set standards and fix limits as a requirement for giving the money. In some states even this system has not been able to meet the needs, and, as in North Carolina with local roads, the state has simply taken over all control and local units have no say in the matter. Financial necessity has overborne ideas of local autonomy, of freedom of action, and has nullified the force of local traditions. While Vermont has not taken any such drastic action, a study of the statutes shows that for many years the state has been forced slowly and reluctantly to assume more and more of the burdens of local government. In fact, about a third of the Vermont towns look to the state for half

231

or more of their local operating costs. The state gives grants-in-aid, carries on state supervision, gives advice, and sometimes assumes functions outright. There is no end in sight for this trend — facts are quite the contrary.

Questions may immediately come to mind. Does this mean that local government is through? Can the town form of government maintain its integrity under modern conditions? What can be done to forestall the loss of local identity? The answers in order may well be a definite, "No," a questioning "Perhaps, but not in the present form," and "Many things." Although these answers do imply a change in current practices, they do not mean that the great principle of self-government will disappear. The structure of local government is human and reasonable, and as such can be changed and improved and still be effective. The citizens of each town will be under the obligation to take advantage of planning commissions, of study groups, of informed voting, and of other opportunities for self-instruction. What may be satisfactory elsewhere may not work in Vermont; what is effective in one section of the state may prove to be impractical elsewhere. Areas and populations are also to be considered. There is no set answer.

A careful weighing of all the factors needs to be made to see if there is any reason why or why not changes should be made. Should town areas be the same? What is a minimum population figure for the most efficient and economical operation of a Vermont town? Can a town with fewer than 100 people, 300 people, or (?) people bear the costs inherent in local government? What is the per capita cost of a town's government, and how does it compare with others? What does the citizen get for his tax money? Does the town really support its own government or is it dependent upon the state, and if so, what excuse is there for its continuation? These are provocative questions and strong answers can be given in support of both sides in a discussion. An emotional display concerning the sanctity of the old town borders will not show how to get the town out of debt. Pointing out the long history of the town will not give the children an adequate school, nor build a single foot of road; both of these enterprises require the outlay of cold cash. There are no Aladdin's lamps to bring a good genie to carry out modern governmental practices.

One thing that man has learned through the years is that when something cannot be accomplished through the efforts of one individual, it may be possible to accomplish it by combining the efforts of many persons. However, the cooperative approach has usually been the last, and sometimes a reluctant effort on the part of unsuccessful doers, and to their amazement has often been the key to success. This is the situation underlying town services. When one person cannot provide for his needs, say for roads, he calls on the community, and the construction is done. It is thus with taxes — no other expenditure made by the ordinary family returns as much to it as its contribution to the mutual enterprise known as government. The cooperation of all makes it possible for each to have more than could be dreamed of otherwise. Let each citizen take his own tax bill, divide it into its component parts, and then decide whether he could get the same services himself for either the separate payment or the total during his taxpaying lifetime.

The strange fact is that while most townspeople see the value of cooperation within the town, few wish to carry the principle over into inter-town cooperation or combinations. The General Assembly has recognized the need for inter-town cooperation and has from time to time sponsored and enacted legislation to help the towns help themselves. The laws permit the joint hiring of town managers, and recent enactments have provided for votes on joint high school districts in which several towns could combine to build, equip, and maintain a good high school in place of the sorry examples that may be found in some towns. The most recent example is the enactment by the General Assembly in 1963, of a statute providing that Vermont towns may voluntarily consolidate if the proposed union has the approval of the two county side judges. Thus the long years of agitation for this action have borne fruit and it will be possible for dying towns to attempt rejuvenation. These approaches to cooperation are wise as they permit differing projects on an experimental basis, and prevent a strait-jacket approach; no coercion is implied since the towns take steps only after a discussion of the program and a public vote on acceptance or rejection. Experimental steps in specific services can provide the understanding and background for final full cooperation.

Cooperation and consolidation would spare declining towns the fate of Glastonbury and Somerset whose local governments were removed by the legislature in 1937. Both of these towns might still be actively participating in self-government if they had long ago united with other towns, instead of waiting until the costs of government had become so high and the services so poor that nearly all the inhabitants had left. It must be remembered that there is no other support for either government or business than the income of the citizens who must spend to live. All payments made in the town by its citizens come from their total income. From this income is taken the money for all their taxes, all their living, and all their savings. If there is no income to tax in the town it is financially insolvent. A single, live, consolidated town is a better argument for democracy than two dead unorganized areas of land.

Governments exist for men, and not men for governments, although totalitarian states follow the latter pattern. Thus the needs of living persons should carry precedence and if a town no longer serves its citizens they have the right to request union with another town, and the other town has the right to say yes or no to the request. History shows that the General Assembly has been willing to combine, or divide, as it thought best for the towns involved. It would seem better for the towns to act voluntarily rather than have an action inflicted upon them. Self-government requires decisions to be made at home, and that is the challenge that faces many towns in Vermont today.

Bibliography

GENERAL LAWS

1. *Laws of the State of Vermont*, Published by Authority, State of Vermont, Rutland, Josiah Fay, 1798. 621, & 205 pp. Always cited as *Vermont Laws of 1797*, because of date of legislative action.
2. The Laws of the *State of Vermont*, Digested and Compiled, Published by order of the Legislature, Vol I and Vol II, Randolph, Sereno Wright, 1808, 505, & 531 pp. Cited as *Laws of Vermont, 1808*.
3. *Laws of the State of Vermont*, to the close of the Session of the Legislature in the year 1816; . . . Vol. III, 336 pp. Rutland, Fay, Davison and Burt, 1817.
4. *The Laws of Vermont*, of a Publick and Permanent Nature: Coming Down to, and Including, the Year 1824. Compiled, By Authority of the Legislature, by Wm. Slade, Jun., 756 pp. 1825, Windsor, Simeion Ide.
5. *The Laws of Vermont*, of a Public and Permanent Nature, Coming Down to, and Including the year 1834. Compiled By Authority of the Legislature, by Daniel P. Thompson, 1835, 228 pp. Montpelier, Knapp and Jewett, 1835.
6. *The Revised Statutes of the State of Vermont*, Published by Order of the Legislature, Burlington, Chauncey Goodrich, 1840, 676 pp.
7. *The Compiled Statutes of the State of Vermont*, Compiled, in Pursuance of an Act of the Legislature, by Charles L. Williams, Burlington, Chauncey Goodrich, 1851, 815 pp.
8. *The General Statutes of the State of Vermont*, Published By the State of Vermont, 1863, 1050 pp.
9. *The General Statutes of the State of Vermont*, Second Edition with an Appendix. Comprising the Public Laws Enacted Since the Annual Session of 1862. Published by the State of Vermont, 1870. 1352 pp.
10. *The Revised Laws of Vermont, 1880*. Published By Authority, Rutland, Tuttle & Co. 1881, 1169 pp.
11. *The Vermont Statutes, 1894*, Published By Authority, Rutland, The Tuttle Company, 1895, 1313 pp.
12. *The Public Statutes of Vermont 1906*, Published By Authority, 1907, 1302 pp., & 380 pp. Index. (Concord, N.H., The Rumford .Printing Company.)

13. *The General Laws of Vermont 1917*, Published By Authority, 1918, 1370 pp. & 203 pp. Index. (Burlington, Free Press Printing Co.)
14. *The Public Laws of Vermont 1933*, Published By Authority, 1934, 1603 pp., & 219 pp. Index. (Montpelier, Capital City Press.)
15. *The Vermont Statutes, Revision of 1947*, Published By Authority, 1947, 2160 pp., & 297 pp. Index.
16. *Vermont Statutes Annotated.* 1958, Orford, N. H., Equity Publishing Corporation, 9 Volumes, Titles 1-33, Index and Tables.

SESSION LAWS

17. Generally, *The Acts and Laws, The Laws,* or the *Acts and Resolves,* enacted by the General Assembly 1779 to 1963. These were issued twice or three times a year in the 18th Century, generally once a year until 1870, and biennially since then.
18. *Acts and Laws of the State of Vermont in American, Passed by the General Assembly of the Representatives of the Freemen of the State of Vermont,* at the Session at Bennington, February 11th, A.D. 1779. Printed by Judah Padock & Alden Spooner, 1779. Dresden, (which is now Hanover, N.H.)

OTHER WORKS

19. Biennial Reports of the Vermont State Board of Education, 1940-1962.
20. *Biennial Report of the Department of Forests and Parks, 1961-62,* and previous reports 1940 to 1960, issued under different titles for the Department.
21. Biennial Reports of the State Highway Board, 1940 - 1962.
22. Carroll, Daniel B., *The Unicameral Legislature of Vermont,* Montpelier, The Vermont Historical Society, 1933.
23. Conant, Edward, *The Geography, History, Constitution, and Civil Government of Vermont,* 5th Ed. Revised and enlarged by Mason Stone, Rutland, Tuttle Publishing Company, 1907.
24. Dunham, Paul C., and Claribel Morton, *A Handbook For Vermont Selectmen,* Burlington, Government Clearing House, (University of Vermont.) 1962.
25. *Governmental Costs and Taxes in 150 Vermont Towns,* Bulletin No. 546, Vermont Agricultural Experiment Station, September 1948.
26. Merrill, Perry H., *Forestry in Vermont, 1947,* No date, no publisher but issued in 1947, for the Forest Festival Week, at the instigation of Governor Gibson.
27. Nuquist, Andrew E., "Freeman's Oath," in *XVI Vermont Quarterly,* (New Series), No. 2, April 1948, pp. 53 - 64.
28. Rossiter, William, "Vermont. An Historical and Statistical Study of the Progress of the State," *American Statistical Association,* New Series, No. 93, March 1911, pp. 387 - 454, with nine maps.
29. *Report of the Treasurer and Auditor of Accounts,* now *Report of the Treasurer and Commissioner of Administration,* issued an-

nually.
30. Sly, John F., *Town Government in Massachusett, 1620 - 1930*, Cambridge, Howard University Press, 1930.
31. Stilwell, Lewis D., *Migration from Vermont*, Montpelier, Vermont Historical Society, 1948.
32. Stone, Mason, *History of Education, State of Vermont, 1777 - 1927*, Montpelier. No publisher and no date, but probably 1930.
33. *The Thirty-Second Vermont School Report*, 1892, Montpelier, 1892.
34. *Vermont Educational Directory*, 1940-41, to 1962-63, Montpelier, Vermont Department of Education.
35. *Vermont Legislative Directory and State Manual*, Biennially, 1941, 1943, etc.
36. *Vermont State Papers*, Compiled and Published by William Slade, Jun., Secretary of State, Middlebury, J.W. Copeland Printer, 1823, 568 pp.

Index

pay for, 34

Diseases, infectious; see Health Officer
need for additional tax rate to

Dislike of government by early Vermonters, 111

Docket
County court — when crowded may require sitting of supreme court judge and one assistant judge, 229
prepared by county clerk as clerk of the court, 212

Dodge, Warren R. (Dick)
Town report contest, officers' schools, xii-xiv

Drainage, land; see Soil conservation districts

Driver's license
must pay poll tax to get, 53

Education; see also School districts
Charter grants, early, 140
constitutional requirement for, in each town, amended in 1955, 140
functions of towns in Vermont, 140
injury by impassible winter roads in past, 142
law of 1782 permitted as many school districts in town as needed by legal vote, 140
school age fixed 1797 at 4 - 18 years, 140

Efficiency; see Town manager

Elections
constable
posts notice for, 104
presides at, 104
number of, for Vermont citizens, 156
of representatives, 166-167
Secretary of State draws up forms for posting notice of, 104

Essex County

regional development in, 184

Essex Junction Village
village forest and its value, cordwood, development, 191

Estray; see Pound keeper

European states
municipal forests in, 192

Executive Council
abolition, people willing to in 1836, 205
acted as justices of the peace, until 1836, 216
found in Constitution of 1777; to aid governor, 204

Expenditures, town
Newport Express editorial calling for, to be concentrated where would do most good, 183

Expenses, town
to be voted. 13

Faculty tax
levied upon professionals in early days, 38-39

Farms
fewer producing more milk in 1962, 174
number of, in Vermont, 173
submarginal, 174
valley, lost to road construction and flood control, 175

Fees
paid to town clerk, 29

Fences; see also Fence viewer
construction of, 116
each owner to pay fair share of costs, 116
when animals move along road, when none along road, 116 116
where must be built, 116

Fences, inadequate
suits for damages when, 117

Fence, spite
prohibited, 117

Fence viewer
general discussion, 115-119

may order sewer connections, 123

member of town board of health, 122

possibility of health officer in union of towns, 123

usually a layman, too few doctors, 123

Hearse warden, 114

High bailiff

arrests sheriff and assumes duties when necessary; o n l y function, 202

Highway commissioner, town; see Road commissioner

Highways, town; see also Roads vote in town meetings on, 14

Hill farms

abandoned, too steep to operate, 174

Hill, Olney W.

Director of public records, better record keeping, 28

Homes

construction, regulation of, under zoning ordinance, 186

Hoop poles; see Culler of Hoop Poles, staves and Headings, 114

Hopkins, Theodore

Burlington City attorney, xii-xiv

Hops; see Inspectors of Hops, 128

House of Representatives

judges, — votes for, from candidates recommended by organized bar, 229

Income tax, state

became chief state tax in 1931, substituted for property tax, 37

Incompatible offices

no one may serve in two, exceptions, 64

overseer included in list, 94

selectmen and town agent, town agent and selectmen, 119

selectmen must prevent holding of, 32

Incorporated school district; see School districts, incorporated nineteen in 1962, 143

Indifferent person

court officer in municipal court, may be, 225

Individual valuation

varying sums, 51

$100 value, 48

Indoor relief; see Relief-Indoor

Industrial wastes

dumping of, regulated by town vote; harmful, 180

Industry, new

bribes to get, 196

cost to towns for, 197

labor price and markets available, 195

number of plants in Vermont amazing, 195

one industry towns not good, 195

raw material determines; shortage of, in Vermont, 195

subsistence farming and industrial employment possible, 195

subsistence farming, values of, and employment, 195-196

tax exemptions, risky to grant, 196

tax exemption votes for, 196

towns may vote bonds to build industrial plant, 196-187

Industrial building construction

by towns, authorized 1955, 196

tax exempt certificate of indebtedness issued, 196

Inefficiency

in spending money, 111

Infectious diseases; see Health officer

Inspectors of flour

formerly chosen by town meeting, duties and fees, 128

Inspectors of hops

serve as, 122

check list, make up, 158

deficits, responsible for restoring, 35

fill vacancies in office of, may, 103

fire districts; to act on petitions for proposed, to fix boundaries of proposed, to issue warning for first meeting of proposed, 134

Handbook for Vermont Selectmen, A, 31

health officer, recommends to State Board of Health, 122

and health officer are town board of health, 122

lawyer, to hire when town agent requests, 119

 may hire when town agent does not, 118

manager, to appoint and supervise a town, when town votes, 33

monument to soldiers and sailors, build and maintain when required, 32

overseer of the poor, act as, or have town elect, 14

 may act as; supervises overseer, 94

parks, lay out, 32

policy forming agency, chief, next to town meeting, 33

roads

 act on petition for new road. 84-85

  if no action by, to county court, 86

 charge of road work, 83

 joint action by boards of selectmen on inter-town roads, 86

make a sworn statement of road mileage in town, 92

 must pay damages for new

roads, 85

public hearing on petition for new roads, 85

state auditor, to warn for calling, 32

state auditor, item for —— to audit town books, 13

tax rate determined by, and presented to town in town report, 33

three in each town, 30

town fire warden, give approval of appointment of, 124-5

warning for town meeting, drawn by and posted, 11

 for town school district meeting, 16

trustees of public funds, 120

zoning commission created by, on vote of town, 184

zoning ordinance drawn up by, hearing on called by 184-5

Selectmen, Board of

organized at close of town meeting, 30

Selectmen, First

usually chairman and in third year of office, 31

Self-government

possible only when all men equal before the law, 230

Senate

age of senators, 206-207

apportionment in 1963, 206

Council of Censors, proposed, in 1834, 205

number of Senators in 1963, 206

popular support for, factors behind, 205

reapportionment called for; failure to do so 1941-1962, 206

size of, 206

temporary act apportioning, 1962, 206

Senator

Qualifications for, 206